PSYCHOANALYSIS ENTERS THE POLITICAL FRAY

*Op-Ed Articles and Journal Blogs
of Peter Wolson*

PSYCHOANALYSIS ENTERS THE POLITICAL FRAY

Op-Ed Articles and Journal Blogs of Peter Wolson

PETER WOLSON, Ph.D.

IPBOOKS.net
International Psychoanalytic Books

International Psychoanalytic Books (IPBooks)
New York
IPBooks.net

International Psychoanalytic Books (IPBooks)
Queens, NY 11104
Online at: IPBooks.net

ISBN: 978-1-949093-14-8

PSYCHOANALYSIS ENTERS THE POLITICAL FRAY

Permissions For Graphics

1. *Eagleton and America's Psychophobia.* Graphic: (Most likely) Yardley Jones; efforts to contact Artist were unsuccessful.

2. *Hating the Politician in the Mirror.* Graphic: Steve McAfee, deceased; efforts to contact the artist's heirs were unsuccessful.

3. *Politics of Victimhood.* Graphic: Tim Teebken; reprinted with the permission of the artist.

4. *Strange To Say, but Neurotics Are Preferable.* Graphic: William Panos: reprinted with the permission of the artist.

5. *When Politics Is Also Psychology.* Graphic: Steve McAfee, deceased; efforts to contact artist's heirs were unsuccessful.

6. *A World of Psychophobia.* Photo of Sigmund Freud; photographer unknown, public domain.

7. *America's State of Mind: Healthy and Divided.* Graphic: Martin Gunsaullus; reprinted with the permission of the artist.

8. *All Our Children: The Inner Appeal Of America's Primal Families.* a. Photo of the Sopranos: Anthony Neste. reprinted with the permission of the photographer. b. Photo of William and Hillary Clinton. Photographer Unknown.

9. *The Politics of Confession.* Graphic: Song and Dance by Susan Tibbles; reprinted with the permission of the artist.

TABLE OF CONTENTS

FOREWORD   *iii*

ACKNOWLEDGMENTS   *v*

CHAPTER I. INTRODUCTION   1

CHAPTER II. CONCEPTUAL STRATEGY FOR WRITING
PSYCHOANALYTIC OP-ED PIECES AND ONLINE BLOGS   13

CHAPTER III. PSYCHOPHOBIA IN RELATION TO THE
MENTALLY ILL, PSYCHOANALYSIS AND STUTTERERS   35

   1.   Eagleton and America's Psychophobia *(Los Angeles Times,* 1972)   37

   2.   A World of Psychophobia *(Los Angeles Times,* 2000)   45

   3.   Is Stuttering Biological or Psychological? A Psychoanalyst's Perspective
      (Huffington Post, 2011).   50

CHAPTER IV. THE INFLUENCE OF PSYCHOLOGICAL
DEVELOPMENT ON PRESIDENTIAL LEADERSHIP   55

   1.   When Politics Is Also Psychology *(Los Angeles Times,* 1999)   56

   2.   The Bush Boys: No Sibling Rivalry, but Maybe Something Deeper
      (Thomson Reuters, 2015)   63

CHAPTER V. THE PSYCHODYNAMICS OF POLITICAL, RACIAL, RELIGIOUS AND MISOGYNISTIC HATRED   67

1. Hating the Politician in the Mirror *(Los Angeles Times,* 1999)   69

2. The "Passion" of Antisemitism (Unpublished, 2004)   75

3. America's State of Mind: Healthy and Divided
   (Los Angeles Times, 2000)   81

4. America's Racism: Hatred of "The Other"
   in the 2008 Presidential Election *(Huffington Post,* 2008)   85

5. The Hatred Between Republicans and Democrats:
   The Conflict Within America's Psyche, Redux *(Huffington Post,* 2008)   89

6. Fiscal Cliff: D.C.'s Mayan Apocalypse *(Thomson Reuters,* 2012)   91

7. Does Dependency on Government Make Americans Weak?
   (Huffington Post, 2012)   95

8. The Puzzling Vilification of Hillary, A Psychoanalyst's Perspective
   (Huffington Post, 2015)   99

CHAPTER VI. THE POLITICAL ALLURE OF BEING "ABOVE THE LAW"   105

1. All Our Children: The Inner Appeal of America's Primal Families
   (Los Angeles Times, 2001)   106

2. The Politics of Confession *(Los Angeles Times,* 2001)   111

3. The Politics of Narcissism: America's Grandiose Persona Under Bush
   (CounterPunch, 2004)   116

CHAPTER VII. ANALYZING SOCIETAL VIOLENCE, CRIMINALITY AND ITS PSYCHOLOGICAL AFTERMATH   121

1. Strange to Say, but Neurotics Are Preferable *(Los Angeles Times*, 1999)   123

2. The Aurora Massacre: Coping With the Precariousness of Human Existence *(Huffington Post*, 2012)   128

3. The Joe Paterno Syndrome: Idealization and the Corruption of Morality *(Huffington Post*, 2011)   133

CHAPTER VIII. THE PSYCHOLOGY OF GENOCIDE AND TORTURE IN WAR   137

1. Politics of Victimhood: A Perpetual Cycle of Abuse *(Los Angeles Times*, 1999)   138

2. The Underlying Dynamic of Post-9/11 America: Exhibitionistic Revenge at Abu Ghraib *(CounterPunch*, 2004)   143

3. Compromising America's Moral Integrity Versus Ensuring Military Support *(Huffington Post*, 2015)   148

CHAPTER IX. PRESIDENT TRUMP, "HIS MAJESTY, THE BABY"   151

1. Trumping Americans: The Strange, Irresistible Appeal of a Narcissistic Bloviator *(Huffington Post*, 2015)   154

2. Trumping American Democracy: The Frightening Rise of a Fascistic Authoritarian *(International Psychoanalysis*, 2015)   160

3. America's "White-Lash" And The Degradation Of Reason *(Huffington Post*, 2017)   165

4. Trump's Narcissism: A Key to His Success and Tragic Flaw *(Huffington Post*, 2017)   172

CHAPTER X. CONCLUSION: "BREAKING NEWS OF THE DAY"—THE ENDURING INFLUENCE OF POLITICAL PSYCHODYNAMICS   181

REFERENCES   203

INDEX   208

ABOUT THE AUTHOR   233

To Margaux Olivia Wolson

The noblest pleasure is the joy of understanding.

–Leonardo da Vinci

FOREWORD

At this time of doubt in the mental health profession regarding what our role should be in the deepening national and international crises, many concerned voices are agitated by the apparent passivity of members and the neutrality of our formal professional organizations. Peter Wolson, a psychoanalyst, gives us a collection of his published (and one unpublished) op-eds, opinion pieces, and memos of the past few years. Whereas many analysts are critical about their profession speaking only to other analysts, Peter has for years been lucidly and appealingly reaching out to the literate public. His writing is well-informed, critical, and pungent. He is generously self-reflective, sharing with sensibility his personal history, pain, and psychodynamics. For example, in his section on the psychological sources of stuttering, he shows how in his own case, being from a divorced broken home and shared custody, unconscious rage caused him to stutter when in the home of one parent but not the other. "As a young child of divorced parents, when I lived with one parent, my stuttering increased, but then virtually disappeared when I lived with the other parent" (see pages 48 and 49).

The center of Peter's concern in this book is the fact that our national leadership from the top down is dominated by pathological narcissism. Donald Trump's narcissism has a manic quality that is a defense against his sense of inadequacy, which he handles by his tweets and interviews, daily putting his injured self into various others, whom he demeans and humiliates with nasty deprecating labels such as "dogs," "low IQ," "low energy," "li'l Marco," and "crooked Hillary." He called CNN journalist Don Lemon "the dumbest man on television!'," "a lightweight," and "dumb as a rock." Donald Trump's arrogance and contempt is a defense against his own feelings of worthlessness and inferiority. In Trump's unconscious, there is a latent awareness of the falsehood and inaccuracy of his claims—for instance, the Barack Obama "birther" fiction, which he promoted to the bitter end. This adds to his underlying anxiety, stress, and feelings of worthlessness. His defense is the adulation of crowds of his admirers who reinforce his sense of special merit and enjoy his projections of worthlessness onto political opponents. His "America First" isolationist arrogance and abrogation of international commitments is an identification of himself with America as morally right and infallible. This leads to sloppiness in decision making without appropriate consideration of the consequences, and an unjustified confidence in the rightness of his decisions.

Peter's agenda is to revitalize the relationship between the mental health profession and the reading public. He writes with the conviction that informed expertise in psychodynamics is relevant, and in fact essential, in comprehending public personalities and civic, national, and international affairs. It is a pleasure to embark with Peter on an open-ended exploration of American politics, personalities, and hot controversial issues.

Peter Loewenberg, Ph.D.
Professor Emeritus, Department of History, UCLA

ACKNOWLEDGEMENTS

I would first like to thank my wife and muse, Margaux, whom I consulted every step of the way. She enriched the book with her perceptive insights, organizational recommendations and meticulous grammatical corrections. This would not have been the same book without her.

I thank my writer father, as my ego ideal, who inspired me to write and whom I have always tried to emulate. But undeniably, my greatest inspiration for writing opinion pieces was Allison Silver, Chief Editor of the *Los Angeles Times* Sunday "Opinion" section. She encouraged me to write for her, and mentored and supported me, even as I struggled with some of the pieces. She and Gary Spiecker, her associate, were marvelous editors, and I benefitted greatly from their suggestions. I also thank her for using me as a psychological consultant to some of her *New York Times* reporters and for editing my *Thomson Reuters* blogs.

I wish to thank Arianna Huffington for making me a blogger for the *Huffington Post*, and also Alexander Cockburn and Jeffrey St. Clair for publishing two of my pieces in *CounterPunch*.

I am extremely grateful to Presidents Otto Kernberg and Stefano Bolognini of the International Psychoanalytical Association for validating my op-ed and blog writing as a significant way for an analyst to contribute a psychoanalytic perspective to the political dialogue in the public media.

In addition, I greatly appreciate psychoanalytic historian Peter Loewenberg's encouragement since I started writing these pieces, as well as the interest of so many psychoanalysts in the Los Angeles community and elsewhere. I am extremely grateful to Peter for writing the Foreword to this book.

I wish to thank Christopher Bollas, my friend Alan Spivak, and Daniel Benveniste for their invaluable suggestions for improving the manuscript. The extremely generous blurbs of Stefano Bolognini, Christopher Bollas, Daniel Benveniste, Vamik Volkan and Steven Ellman are more than I could have wished for.

In addition, I thank Annie Babin for her creative brilliance in designing the book cover and Kathy Kovacic of Blackthorn Studio for her beautiful interior design. I am also grateful to the following graphic artists of the *Los Angeles Times* op-ed pieces: William Panos, Susan Tibbles, Anthony Neste and Tim Teebken, for granting their permission to use their art in this book. I also wish to thank editorial artists Steve McAfee, Yardley Jones and Martin Gunsaullus. Erica Varela, the *Los Angeles Times* copyright editor and Elena Novikova of the *Toronto Sun* provided invaluable counsel in researching copyright permissions. And I am indebted to Allen Hyman, my friend and attorney, who conducted a meticulous investigation of copyright entitlements.

Last but certainly not least, I thank Arnold Richards for his unstinting belief in this book and enthusiasm in publishing it through IPBooks. His associates, Tamar Schwartz and Larwence Schwartz, have been indispensible in guiding me through the publication process. Leonard Rosenbaum has been an invaluable copy editor and indexer. I am grateful to everyone who has believed in the importance of deepening the political discourse with a psychoanalytic perspective and who has encouraged me to continue writing about issues that affect all of us so profoundly.

Chapter I █

INTRODUCTION

With the continuous traumatic aftershocks of the Trump presidency, so many Americans, especially Democrats and Independents, are experiencing "politicalitis": overwhelming anxiety, nihilistic despair and a catastrophic apprehension that they are witnessing the destruction of all they have prized about American democracy. There has never been a more critical time than now for psychoanalysts to contribute their knowledge of unconscious psychodynamic processes that motivate and shape political events, to enrich and deepen the public dialogue about the current state of our union. On the listserve of Division 39 (Psychoanalysis) of the American Psychological Association, many analysts have been champing at the bit to join the political fray. This, along with our current political climate, has inspired me to write this book.

In Amsterdam, at the Plenary Session of the 40th Congress of the International Psychoanalytical Association in 1997, Otto Kernberg urged psychoanalysts throughout the world to enter public forums and to demonstrate the importance of psychoanalysis and the practical utility of psychoanalytic understanding in dealing with political and cultural events. Psychoanalysts have always yearned to expand their contribution to humanity beyond the couch by applying their knowledge of unconscious psychodynamics to society at large, but this longing has become more pressing since 9/11.

Journalists and "talking heads" are continually psychologizing about political personalities and events, usually without the psychoanalytic background to make the most informed conjectures. They are typically "winging it." Unfortunately, there have been only a handful of psychoanalysts in America, such as the late Leo Rangell, Jonathan Lear, Todd Essig, Robert Stolorow, and a few others, who have entered this public arena. In contrast, European and Argentinian psychoanalysts have had a long tradition of offering psychoanalytic perspectives for the public in newspapers and magazines.

One way to contribute to the dialogue is by writing psychoanalytically-informed op-ed pieces and blogs. Over the past 43 years, I have published 25 articles in newspapers and online journals: nine op-ed pieces in the Sunday "Opinion" section of the *Los Angeles Times,* eleven online blogs in the *Huffington Post,* two in *CounterPunch,* two in *Thomson Reuters* and one in *International Psychoanalysis.* My most recent pieces have focused on Donald Trump and Hillary Clinton during and after their 2015/2016 presidential campaigns.

The traditional argument against writing op-ed pieces and blogs has been that it is not neutral or scientific, and therefore not psychoanalytic. This is certainly true of analysts who merely want to advocate their own personal political position without employing psychoanalytic constructs to illuminate the underlying psychodynamics. One might favor the Democrats or Republicans, but explain the political psychodynamics through a psychoanalytic lens that explores the issues while supporting their perspective. If the interpretations are correct, the public might react like most patients, with surprise and recognition of their validity. The important contribution is that analytic insight deepens the discussion.

Thus, the analyst's goal would be to illuminate the unconscious processes involved in the political/cultural event and speculate about the consequences of that analytic understanding. Regardless of what the analyst might conclude, he or she would not discard an objective, empirical perspective. The politically engaged analyst would be educating the public about unconscious processes and their powerful influence on human activities. I believe this would make psychoanalysis more relevant to the public, which often tends to view psychoanalysis as an effete, arcane profession. Through online digital technology, we are increasingly empowered to make psychoanalysis more relevant to the public.

For example, some of my pieces have advocated particular points of view. "Eagleton and America's Psychophobia" (1972), "A World of Psychophobia" (2000), and "Is Stuttering Biological or Psychological?" (2011) were intended to fight psychophobia, the pervasive fear of the unconscious and the psychological. But most of my pieces have primarily revealed the unconscious psychodynamics motivating political issues without advocating a political position.

Sigmund Freud utilized psychoanalysis to explain unconscious political and cultural psychodynamics in various writings, as did D. W. Winnicott, Erik Erikson, Nevitt Sanford, Theodor Adorno, Else Frenkel-Brunswick, Daniel Levinson, Abram Kardiner, Geza Roheim, Ruth Benedict and Harold Lasswell, to name a few. More recently, Vamik Volkan, Leo Rangell, Eli Zaretsky and Christopher Bollas have done the same. A number of psychoanalytic journals have been devoted to political, cultural and historical issues.

In contrast to writing for a professional audience, my psychoanalytic political pieces have been written for the American public. Some colleagues have questioned the legitimacy of this kind of psychoanalytic writing. But I felt reassured when Otto Kernberg (President of the IPA at the time), after reading a few of my op-eds, wrote, "I am very grateful for the articles you sent me, a response to the bias against psychoanalysis in the press, and in support of the relevance of psychoanalysis for mental care and social issues at this time. I very much agree that we need to continue spelling out the importance of psychoanalysis to the American public, and you certainly have contributed in a significant way" (June 13, 2000). He was reacting to "A World of Psychophobia" (May 28, 2000), an op-ed piece (published in the *Los Angeles Times)* that addressed the criticism of psychoanalysis that was triggered by a travelling exhibit on Sigmund Freud. Dr. Kernberg's encouragement strengthened my conviction that this type of writing was a legitimate and important way to demonstrate the unique contribution of psychoanalytic understanding for contemporary society. More recently, Dr. Stefano Bolognini, past-president of the International Psychoanalytical Association, echoed this sentiment in an email: "My feeling is that you opened a new important door in the cultural area of our community" (March 6, 2017).

In this book, I will demonstrate how seminal unconscious psychodynamic conflicts, motivations, defenses and developmental processes motivate political (and cultural) events and inevitably repeat themselves in varying political contexts over time, a form of "repetition compulsion," if you will. I fervently hope that this book will inspire other psychoanalysts and kindred professionals (psychologists, psychiatrists, clinical social workers, marriage family therapists, nurse practitioners, pastoral counselors, psychoanalytically-oriented historians, political scientists, sociologists, journalists, criminologists, anthropologists and behavioral economists) who are intellectually involved in politics and history, to write psychoanalytically informed op-ed pieces and blogs for the media on the "breaking news of the day."

My Background for Political Writing

I grew up in the Bronx and Long Island, New York, in a Russian Jewish, left-wing household. My grandparents fled the Ukrainian pogroms to America, and my parents were both first generation. My mother was a high school art teacher, and my father, a pulp fiction detective-story writer who fought in the Lincoln Brigade against Franco in the Spanish Civil War. The radio was always turned on to news programs, and my father and I discussed political and cultural issues routinely. He was a divergent thinker, and he constantly provoked me into using my imagination and speculating "out-of-the-box." When his side of my family got together, the political discussions were so loud that you could barely hear what anyone was saying. This intellectual, argumentative atmosphere stimulated my political curiosity, and encouraged me to assert my own point of view. At CCNY, I joined the debating society and wanted to become a lawyer, but eventually chose psychology, finding it more meaningful.

I never envisioned writing political opinion articles. In fact, I was more oriented toward writing fiction like my father or painting like my mother. My attraction to psychotherapy was influenced, in part, by my expectation of hearing interesting personal dramas that might be material for writing fiction. But during my psychotherapy training, I became passionate about exploring the complexities of the human psyche, and my desire to write fiction waned.

Writing op-ed pieces was the furthest from my mind in August 1972, and I never anticipated that this would happen to me. I was working as a staff psychologist at St. John's Hospital in Santa Monica, California, when I read a news article about the shocking disclosure of the psychiatric history of Senator Thomas Eagleton, who was the Democratic vice presidential candidate. A reporter had discovered that Eagleton had been hospitalized for depression and had received electroshock treatments (ECT). A political outcry ensued, condemning him for his poor judgment for not having previously revealed these "psychological skeletons in his closet." While America was in the thick of the Cold War and fighting the Viet Cong, politicians and pundits became alarmed. How could Americans trust a "psycho" a heartbeat away from the Presidency with the possibility of igniting a nuclear holocaust?

I became incensed. Senator Eagleton had been a highly popular, charismatic, effective senator from Missouri, which was why Democratic presidential nominee George McGovern had chosen him as his running mate. But now that his mental illness had been exposed, the public's "psychophobia" ruled the day. I was angry at the widespread discrimination against the mentally ill, and spent the afternoon writing what became my first op-ed piece. I mailed the article to the chief editor of the *Los Angeles Times'* Sunday "Opinion" section, doubting that I would hear back. But a few days later, I received a letter informing me that the article had been accepted, and I would be receiving a check for $150. I was elated.

The article was published the following Sunday almost exactly as I had written it, entitled "Eagleton and America's Psychophobia" (see page 37). It was accompanied by a cartoon featuring a sophisticated-looking male bus rider reading a newspaper with the front-page headline: US VICE PRESIDENTIAL CANDIDATE ADMITS PSYCHIATRIC CARE. The subtitle of the cartoon read: "Frankly, I'm more concerned about certain politicians who have NOT had psychiatric treatment."

This validation of psychotherapy was more than I could hope for. When I recovered from my euphoria, I became apprehensive about my job. As a staff psychologist at St. John's Hospital, which was mentioned in the byline, I was concerned about the reaction of the Catholic nun administrators who employed me. In this piece, I had taken a strong stand on Eagleton's right to lie about his psychiatric record. This was because the social stigma of his mental illness would have probably ruined his chances of being nominated vice-president.

Monday morning, my anxiety peaked when the clinic secretary informed me that the chief administrator of the hospital was waiting for me in the reception room. With trepidation, I approached a middle-aged, bespectacled nun wearing a habit. To my astonishment, she greeted me with a broad smile and shook my hand. "Congratulations! Good job." In retrospect, I recalled that Catholic organizations like hers, the Sisters of Charity of Leavenworth, were renowned for helping the poor, the disabled and the mentally ill.

Prior to this, I had interned at Mount Zion Hospital's psychoanalytic clinic in San Francisco and completed a psychoanalytically-oriented postdoctoral fellowship at the University of Colorado Medical Center in Denver. But I had not yet chosen to become a psychoanalyst. After writing the Eagleton article, I mistakenly concluded that I had to feel passionately about a news event that directly involved a psychological issue before writing another piece. Twenty-seven years elapsed before publishing my next article.

By 1999, I had become a training and supervising analyst at the Los Angeles Institute and Society for Psychoanalytic Studies (LAISPS) and was in private practice in Beverly Hills. The Republican House of Representatives' attempt to impeach President Bill Clinton upset and puzzled me. I wondered why Republicans would display such virulent hatred toward the most conservative of all Democratic presidents. Clinton had implemented highly conservative policies, to the chagrin of many Democrats.

Two psychoanalytic constructs seemed to explain the Republicans' vitriol: Freud's "narcissism of minor differences" and "the superego in the service of the id" (see pages 69–72). On Friday, a few days after submitting this piece to the *Times'* Sunday Opinion section, I received a call from the editorial assistant of Allison Silver, the Chief Editor, informing me that it had been rejected. Over the weekend, I wondered where to send it next, when on Sunday, Allison Silver called me at home. She said she was interested in the article, and asked if I would make some minor changes and have it back to her by Tuesday. I complied with her request On the following Sunday I opened the *Times'* Opinion section, and there was my second published op-ed piece after a 27-year hiatus.

"Hating the Politician in the Mirror, (1999)" was accompanied by a graphic image of Bill Clinton's face as the bull's eye in a circular mirror that resembled a target impaled by darts (see page 69). Like the Eagleton piece, this was written in the political moment. After Allison published it, she said she would like me to think of writing other pieces from a psychological perspective, and that if she didn't hear from me within three months, she would call to see if I had other ideas. Her secretary let me know how rare it was to be in this position based on an unsolicited submission. The *Times'* Sunday "Opinion" section featured op-ed pieces from the most politically and culturally influential people in the world and from columnists who earned their living writing op-ed pieces. I felt exceptionally lucky to share the same pages with them.

I didn't wait to submit more pieces to Allison, and she gave me ideas of her own, such as the pride of victimhood in the Serbians' mentality during their genocidal war with Albanian Muslims, and analyzing Al Gore and George W. Bush's childhood experience of fathering and how that might affect their capacity for presidential leadership. She rejected some of my pieces, but accepted most of them. I had to write them quickly to be timely with the "breaking news," and rewrote a number of them to meet her approval. She and her assistant, Gary Spiecker, edited all of my *Times'* pieces.

Before resigning from the Los Angeles Times and becoming editor for the Sunday New York Times' "Week in Review" section, Allison published seven more of my op-eds. These included "Politics of Victimhood: A Perpetual Cycle of Abuse" (1999), about the psychology of victimhood and genocide in Milošević's Serbia; "Strange to Say, but Neurotics are Preferable" (1999), concerning the outbreak of violence in America following the Columbine massacre; "When Politics Is Also Psychology" (1999), reflecting the childhood influence of Bush and Gore's fathers referred to earlier; "America's State of Mind: Healthy and Divided" (2000), in regard to the political gridlock that divided Republicans and Democrats, which obviously still plagues us; "A World of Psychophobia" (2000), described earlier; "All Our Children: The Inner Appeal of America's Primal Families" (2001), exploring the popularity of the Clinton's leaving the White House and The Sopranos in its second season, based on the political allure of acting "above the law"; and "The Politics of Confession" (2001), regarding the adverse consequences of Congressman Gary Condit's unwillingness to accept responsibility for his sexual transgressions with the missing and murdered Chandra Levy. The op-ed titles I chose were discarded and replaced by ones created by the Times' editorial staff. This was their standard practice.

The Sunday *Times* was distributed throughout the United States and in foreign countries. Some of my pieces were franchised and published by newspapers in other cities. For example, while visiting cousins in Livermore, California, I saw an article of mine in a local newspaper.

As editor of the "Week in Review" and later "Style" section, Allison occasionally told her reporters to call me for a psychological perspective on their topics. I was quoted in four of their articles, one on the psychological value of idealizing a presidential leader, George W. Bush at the time; another on "Gay marriage jitters"; a third on manifestations of repressed sexuality in a children's book, "The Lonely Doll"; and a fourth on Generation X.

I now know how fortunate I was to have caught Allison's attention, as well as that of the first Times editor who published the Eagleton piece. I was able to establish connections with other editors of online journals such as *CounterPunch* and the Huffington Post. For Alexander Cockburn's and Jeffrey St. Clair's *CounterPunch,* I published "The Politics of Narcissism: America's Grandiose Persona Under Bush" (2004), in which I compared the Bush administration to a narcissistic personality disorder, and "The Underlying Dynamic in Post-9/11 America: Exhibitionistic Revenge at Abu Ghraib" (2004), on the humiliating torture of Iraqi prisoners by American soldiers.

Around this time, I met Arianna Huffington at a Los Angeles celebration for liberal columnist Robert Scheer, hosted by *The Nation* magazine, and she made me a blogger for the *Huffington Post* (HP). All together, I published 11 blogs for HP. These were: "America's Racism:

Hatred of 'The Other' in the 2008 Presidential Election" (2008), "The Hatred Between Republicans and Democrats: The Conflict Within America's Psyche, Redux" (2008), "Is Stuttering Biological or Psychological?" (2011), "The Joe Paterno Syndrome: Idealization and the Corruption of Morality" (2011), "The Aurora Massacre: Coping With the Precariousness of Human Existence" (2012), "Does Dependency on Government Make American's Weak? A Psychoanalyst's Perspective" (2012), "Compromising America's Moral Integrity Versus Ensuring Military Support" (2015), "Trumping Americans: The Strange, Irresistible Appeal of a Narcissistic Bloviator" (2015), "The Puzzling Vilification of Hillary, A Psychoanalyst's Perspective" (2016), "Trump's Narcissism: A Key to His Success and Tragic Flaw" (2017), and "America's "White-Lash" and the Degradation of Reason (2017)." I also published "Trumping American Democracy: The Frightening Rise of a Fascistic Authoritarian," (2016) in *International Psychoanalysis*.

For the *Huffington Post*, I had ready access to publishing new pieces until they recently revoked this privilege for their bloggers. None of my blogs for *CounterPunch* or the *Huffington Post* were edited. When Allison Silver became Senior Chief Editor at Thomson Reuters, she published and edited "The Fiscal Cliff: D.C.'s Mayan Apocalypse" (2012) and "The Bush Boys: No Sibling Rivalry, but Maybe Something Deeper" (2015). In addition to these pieces, I have included an unpublished op-ed article on the psychodynamics of anti-Semitism, triggered by Mel Gibson's film, *The Passion of the Christ*.

The structure of this book is organized around the pieces listed above, all of which are included in their entirety with a commentary immediately following. The graphic art that accompanied each of the *Los Angeles Times'* articles is also included. The chapters are written about articles that contain similar political/psychodynamic themes. These themes are (1) psychophobia in relation to the mentally ill, psychoanalysis and stutterers; (2) the influence of psychological development on presidential leadership; (3) the psychodynamics of political, racial, religious and misogynistic hatred; (4) the political allure of being "above the law"; (5) the psychological impact of violence, criminality and its psychological aftermath; (6) the psychology of genocide and torture in war; (7) the psychodynamics of Trump and his influence on America; and (8) "Breaking News of the Day," the enduring relevance of political psychodynamics as history continues to repeat itself.

In this book, I discuss the psychological implications of the psychodynamic constructs within each article for our changing political landscape.

Trump's shocking presidency is galvanizing intense interest among psychoanalysts and other mental health and allied professionals in writing political opinion pieces. It is important to remember that apart from adding psychological depth to the political dialogue, a psychoanalytic perspective has the unique value of transcending any one political or cultural issue and can be applied to a wide variety of human events and experiences. The following chapter describes my conceptual strategy for writing these pieces.

Chapter II |

CONCEPTUAL STRATEGY FOR WRITING PSYCHOANALYTIC OP-ED PIECES AND ONLINE BLOGS

The unique contribution of psychoanalyzing current political and cultural events is through illuminating the deeper, unconscious psychodynamics that underlie and motivate these societal occurrences. My central operating principle is the belief that political and cultural activities are motivated by psychodynamics that are analogous to the internal dynamics of an individual. Beginning with Freud, this principle has been productively applied in an enormous body of interdisciplinary research conducted over the last century within the fields of psychoanalysis (Sigmund Freud, Abram Kardiner, Geza Roheim, Erik Erikson, Vamik Volkan and Leo Rangell) cultural anthropology (Margaret Mead, Ruth Benedict, Franz Boas, Ralph Linton) political science (Harold Lasswell), social psychology (Nevitt Sanford, Ruth Else Frankel-Brunswick, Theodore Adorno, Daniel Levinson), philosophy (Jonathan Lear) and psycholinguistics (George Lakoff).

Historical Precedent

Psychoanalyzing politics and culture appears to have originated with Freud through his explorations of history, art, literature, mythology and archeology. Freud wrote about the psychological motivations of Moses and the nature of Egyptian civilization (1939), Leonardo da Vinci (1910), and creative writers (1908). He used mythology to formulate psychological theories of the Oedipus complex and the role of narcissism in childhood and later development.

In addition, he applied his psychoanalytic acumen to sociological and anthropological subjects. In *Civilization and Its Discontents* (1908), he theorized that human beings unconsciously created civilization to defend against potentially destructive sexual and aggressive impulses in order to interact in society harmoniously. Similarly, in *Totem and Taboo* (Freud, 1913), he hypothesized that the adaptive resolution of the Oedipal conflict in his conception of the "primal horde" was an archaic model for instituting human morality and laws against incest, patricide and infanticide. This ensured the cohesiveness and durability of the human family. He also hypothesized that the "narcissism of minor differences" among various cultures and ethnic groups could trigger the most virulent forms of aggression, including genocide (Freud, 1918, 1921, 1930), and that the devastating brutality of World War 1 was evidence of a powerful aggressive instinct in human nature (1920). Freud's clinical practice was profoundly informed by his fascination with disparate aspects of human experience. His consulting offices in Vienna and London were replete with ancient artifacts that served as imaginative stimuli for his psycho-archeological excavations of buried memories and unconscious psychodynamics.

Freudian psychoanalysis not only influenced critical thinking in literature, politics, art and architecture, but also had a powerful impact on the field of cultural anthropology, whose core concern during the first half of the 20th century was the relationship between personality and culture (Singer, 1961; Kardiner, 1939; Roheim, 1934). Margaret Mead's, *Coming of Age in Samoa* (1928) and Ruth Benedict's *Patterns of Culture* (1934) were seminal examples of this trend. In *Patterns of Culture*, Benedict explored American Indian tribes, concluding that each tribe had its own unique constellation of personality traits. In the Foreword to this book, Margaret Mead said Benedict's thesis was "culture as personality, writ large." Benedict wrote, "A culture, like an individual, is a more or less consistent pattern of thought and action." Each culture unconsciously selected from "the great arc of human potentialities" a few personality traits that became the main characteristics of individuals in that society. Through cross-cultural analyses employing Nietzsche's Apollonian and Dionysian diagnostic criteria, Benedict found that the Pueblo Indian tribes, like the Zuni and Hopi, were more Apollonian—orderly, constrained and somewhat depressed. In contrast, the tribes of the southwest plains, like the Apache, were Dionysian—wild, carefree and paranoid. She went so far as to characterize the Kwakiutl of the Pacific Northwest as "megalomaniacs." Benedict concluded that psychological normality was culturally relative. One could not reasonably judge normality based on universal criteria because each culture had its own unique personality configuration. What was normal in one society might be "crazy" in another. And, of course, not every member fit the defining configuration.

Franz Boas and his students, Ruth Benedict and Margaret Mead, became advocates of the "configurational approach" to culture and personality. According to this perspective, one could not differentiate culture from personality, nor could one accurately assess causal factors of a society's median personality since culture and personality were inextricably intertwined.

In contrast, psychoanalyst Abram Kardiner (heavily influenced by the work of Benedict and Mead) and cultural anthropologist Ralph Linton identified two causal agents of a culture's personality: (1) socioeconomic limitations and child-rearing practices and (2) expressions of artistic, religious and folklore mores. They believed that both factors contribute to the personality of the society, which then becomes a link between these two cultural processes.

Erik Erikson integrated the libidinal dynamics of Freud's instinct-based psychosexual stages with eight sociocultural phases of psychological development. He expanded Freud's schema beyond the genital stage into later adolescence, middle age and old age. His conceptualization enriched the theory of instinctual conflict by making interpersonal psychodynamics primary motivational determinants.

Like Freud, Erikson psychoanalyzed prominent historical figures. In *Young Man Luther: A Study in Psychoanalysis and History* (1958), he analyzed how Martin Luther resolved his conflict between ego identity and role confusion (Erikson's fifth stage of development) by advancing a new conception of man's relationship to God that led to the Protestant Reformation. In his Pulitzer Prize/National Book Award winner, *Gandhi's Truth: The Origins of Militant Nonviolence* (1969), Erikson interpreted Gandhi's passive resistance as masking unconscious violent tendencies, and believed that he resolved his identity crisis of generativity vs. stagnation through founding a new religious and political movement that freed India from British colonial rule.

During World War II, Erikson psychoanalyzed (for the US Military) the German national character and Hitler's charismatic appeal to German youth. The US military also commissioned Nevitt Sanford, Else Frankel-Brunswick, Theodore Adorno and David Levinson to investigate the personalities of Hitler and Mussolini. Based upon previous research from such analysts as Erich Fromm and psychoanalytically-inspired Marxist philosopher Herbert Marcuse, this culminated in their classic work, *The Authoritarian Personality* (1950). Also commissioned by the military, Ruth Benedict investigated the Japanese personality in *The Chrysanthemum and the Sword* (1946), based on Japanese-Americans.

Arguably, the most powerful advocate for psychoanalytic political

writing was Professor Harold Lasswell (1930), a renowned political sci-
entist and communications theorist. Lasswell studied psychoanalysis
in Vienna and Berlin and was analyzed by Theodore Reik. He introduced Freudian psychoanalysis to the social sciences by applying Freud's
structural theory (ego–id–superego) to the content analysis of political
problems. Like the cultural anthropologists mentioned above, he used
unconscious intrapsychic conflicts of the individual to explain problems
of society, and was credited with founding the field of political psychology.
Coincidentally, his major research during World War II was conducted
during the same period that Ruth Benedict, Margaret Mead and Abram
Kardiner were exploring the relationship between culture and personality, and when Nevitt Sanford, Theodore Adorno, et. al. were researching
the authoritarian personality.

Another noteworthy contribution during this period was W.J. Cash's
The Mind of the South (1941), a brilliant, controversial analysis in which
Cash employed psychoanalytic constructs to explain the unconscious historical roots of Southern behavior. Cash, who had been a Southern journalist and novelist, wrote columns in local newspapers against the KKK
and Nazi spies. However, the latter had infiltrated New York City and
Mexico City in large numbers, and while visiting Mexico City a few weeks
after publishing *Mind of the South*, Cash told his wife that Nazis were
following him. Shortly after, he was found hanging by his necktie from
a bathroom door hook in his hotel room. The killer was never identified.

More recently, Eli Zaretsky, in *Political Freud* (2015), writing from
a socialist—Enlightenment perspective, revealed the profound historical influence of psychoanalysis on world culture, economics, progressive political movements, lifestyle and psychotherapy. And Christopher
Bollas, in *Meaning and Melancholia* (2018), creatively applied object
relations theory to historical and contemporary politics and culture.

The importance of applied psychoanalysis is reflected in a number of psychoanalytic journals, including *The International Journal
of Applied Psychoanalytic Studies, Imago, American Imago, Journal of*

Applied Psychoanalytic Studies, Organizational and Social Dynamics, and *Psychoanalysis and History.* These journals contain complex, professional papers and are intended for a professional audience. In contrast, psychoanalytically informed op-ed pieces and blogs must be simple and clear enough for the lay public to understand them without having to struggle with complex psychoanalytic theorizing and jargon. Such opinion pieces are not intended to cover the intricate academic nuances of any given topic. They are intended to contribute an effective, comprehensible psychoanalytic perspective to deepen and enrich the political dialogue.

Leo Rangell, Jonathan Lear, Robert Stolorow, and Todd Essig are among the few American psychoanalysts who have written op-ed pieces and online blogs for the public. I would also add George Lakoff, a psycholinguist whose theories involve political object relations constructs. There might be others, but the number is small.

Leo Rangell wrote some blogs for the *Huffington Post.* His major work, *The Mind of Watergate* (1980), focused on the Nixon administration's "compromise of integrity." Rangell discussed what he called "the Nixon Syndrome." He diagnosed this as a lapse in the conscience of America's superego, as indicated by America's tolerant acceptance of the unethical, criminal behavior of Nixon and his administration. Moreover, Vamik Volkan co-authored a psychobiography (1997) and other books on Nixon.

Similarly, in an article for *The New Republic,* Jonathan Lear (1998), a philosophy professor and psychoanalyst, addressed the public and congressional animosity toward President Clinton for his sexual affairs. Lear based his analysis on Freud's mythic conception of the primal horde, in which the dominating primordial father possessed all the women in his family, but was ultimately defeated by his Oedipally competitive sons. Citing this Freudian theory, Lear concluded that Clinton had to be punished for his Oedipal transgressions to preserve the moral principles of American society. In another piece for *The New Republic,* Lear (1995) defended the value of psychoanalysis against its critics and won the Gravida award for this article. (See also Wolson, "A World of Psychophobia," (page 45).

I described similar acts of hubris in an op-ed piece about Clinton's presidency (page 106). Such lapses in conscience are rampant today in President Trump's administration (see Wolson, page 172), in which large swaths of Americans are willing to tolerate President Trump's lying, retribution against perceived enemies, apparent attempts to obstruct justice, possible collusion with Russia, unwillingness to eradicate financial conflicts of interest, draconian separation of immigrant children from their mothers in his "zero tolerance" policy, and impulsive Tweetstorms. Trump and his administration have promulgated an unscrupulous strategy in which the end justifies the means: a willingness to forego reason, ethics and morality to achieve one's goals. These are symptoms of a regression from mature political cooperation to primitive, hateful identity politics (see Wolson, page 165).

Intersubjective/existential psychoanalyst Robert Stolorow has written blogs in *Psychology Today* on existential trauma, such as Americans' reactions to the tragedy of 9/11. He often integrates Heidegger's philosophy with psychoanalytic understanding. In addition, Professor George Lakoff (1996), a renowned Berkeley psycholinguist, theorized that the Republican and Democratic parties represent parental imagos in the American psyche. For him, the Republican ideology symbolizes a strict, moralistic father persona, whereas the Democratic Party symbolizes a warm, nurturing maternal presence. I was unfamiliar with this when I proposed a similar theory from a psychoanalytic perspective. In 2000, toward the end of the Bush/Gore presidential campaign, when the balance of power between the two major parties was 50–50, I published "America's State of Mind: Healthy and Divided" in the *Los Angeles Times*. In this op-ed, I focused on the father and mother personas of the two parties, but saw Republicans as representing autonomy and Democrats representing dependency. The intrapsychic conflict between these two basic human motives seemed to be represented in the body politic as a conflict within the American psyche. During the 2008 presidential election between Senators McCain and Obama, I elaborated this thesis in a piece for the *Huffington Post* (Wolson, 2008).

Like Otto Kernberg, I believe that psychoanalysts need to help the public understand the enormous value of psychoanalytic understanding for treating psychological problems as well as comprehending the complexities of human nature. The Sunday *New York Times* recently produced an op-ed series, called "Couch," which was a marvelous showcase for psychoanalysis and psychotherapy, featuring poignant clinical vignettes. But unfortunately, it was discontinued.

In summary, there is a substantial precedent for psychoanalyzing political and cultural events. The scabrous behavior of President Trump and his administration has motivated many psychoanalysts to want to enlighten the American people about Trump's state of mind. In fact, the widespread noxious influence of Trump's presidency has transformed the American public into a nation of "psychologists," defensively diagnosing his psychological motivations at every turn to prepare themselves for any traumatic consequences of his administration. With this desperate contemporary need for understanding, what stops American psychoanalysts from entering the political fray?

Psychoanalysts' Resistance to Public Media Writing

It Violates Professional Standards of Neutrality, Anonymity and Abstinence

Arguably, the greatest objection to writing for the media is that it violates the clinical analytic attitude of neutrality, anonymity and abstinence. By writing op-ed pieces, the analyst is violating neutrality and anonymity by expressing a personal opinion in a public forum, albeit through a psychoanalytic lens, and violating abstinence by gratifying the analyst's need to impact the political dialogue.

Another consideration is its effect on patients. If a patients knows you are writing such articles and reads them, wouldn't that limit their freedom to express themselves in therapy, and, if so, wouldn't that potentially reduce the effectiveness of treatment? Personally, I have not found this to be the case. In my 45 years of doing this type of writing, some patients have discovered that I write opinion pieces, but only one has objected. But this became grist for the mill, and we were able to work it through therapeutically. Others have been envious, or jealous, for example, fearing that I love writing more than them. Some patients have avoided "googling" my articles, to preserve their positive view of me and protect the analytic process. Some want to know nothing about me, and others want to know everything. But this, of course, is part of the work. Public visibility will evoke transference responses that can deepen the psychoanalytic treatment process. But some patients, if they know you write publicly, might not choose to see you. For others, this issue might remain an unspoken barrier and might lead to an irresolvable impasse and/or destroy the analysis.

It is important to realize that the rules of neutrality, anonymity and abstinence are relative at best. As analysts, we are not merely talking heads. Through everything we do, we are disclosing our personalities. And although patients might see our idiosyncrasies, they will project their transferences onto us anyway. In fact, therapeutic chemistry is often based on having been unconsciously selected as a therapist because we resemble bad and/or good internal objects with which the patient intuitively needs to engage in order to work through problems. If there is a sufficient working alliance and therapeutic transference relationship, I believe the patient's awareness of media writing is unlikely to inhibit or destroy the analysis.

Of course, most of Freud's patients knew he was famous and knew his opinions about various subjects. This might have dissuaded some from wanting to see him while attracting others. Should Freud have rejected interviews with journalists to preserve his anonymity? Similarly, Otto Kernberg, in *Borderline Conditions and Pathological Narcissism* (1975), cites vignettes in which patients responded to his prominence and travels with envious fantasies, which became essential clinical material in treatment.

The Goldwater Rule

The American Psychiatric Association and the American Psychological Association warn their members not to publicly diagnose a living president or any politician or public figure in absentia without their consent. This edict, which became known as the Goldwater rule, was institutionalized by the American Psychiatric Association in 1973, nine years after 1189 psychiatrists signed a petition declaring presidential nominee Barry Goldwater mentally unfit to be president of the United States during his 1964 presidential campaign against Lyndon Johnson. The petition was published in *FACT* magazine. Senator Goldwater successfully sued the magazine for libel, which had to pay him a $75,000 fine. Today this would be equivalent to approximately $625,000. The American Psychological Association agreed with this rule in 2016 in response to public and professional pressure to diagnose Donald Trump's aberrant behavior. The ethical rationale for the Goldwater rule was that diagnosing a person in absentia without their consent would be an unfair violation of their privacy and, at best, a highly speculative assessment based on secondary-source media descriptions.

Many psychiatrists and psychologists, including myself, oppose the Goldwater rule because it prevents us from sharing our diagnostic expertise with the American public. In contrast, non–mental health professionals, including the media and the public, are free to diagnose politicians as they choose. This raises the question, When a living politician's psychological condition adversely affects the mental health of the citizenry and the functioning of government (e.g., Nixon and his administration during the Watergate scandal and the current scandal-ridden Trump administration) or threatens the safety of our nation (e.g,. the potential for nuclear war with North Korea), shouldn't mental health experts help Americans to understand what might be psychologically affecting the President and to understand the potential political ramifications? Wouldn't it be unethical to withhold such professional wisdom, especially if a president's erratic behavior could lead to a preventable nuclear holocaust?

Leo Rangell (1980), President Emeritus of the IPA, disregarded the Goldwater rule and analyzed the criminal mentality of the Nixon administration in his book *The Mind of Watergate*. I have published op-eds for the *Los Angeles Times* analyzing President Clinton's tendency to violate professional ethics and act "above the law." In other pieces, I have speculated about the possible psychological influence of George W.'s and Al Gore's fathers on their capacity for presidential leadership, analyzed the political consequences of Congressman Gary Condit's refusal to confess his extramarital affair with Chandra Levy, and speculated about the psychodynamics of Jeb Bush's inhibition about disagreeing with his brother George W.'s Iraq policy while seeking the Republican Party's nomination.

In my opinion, the presidency of Donald Trump has made the Goldwater rule obsolete. Psychoanalysts, psychiatrists and psychologists are pressuring their national organizations to abolish the Goldwater rule while many of them, including myself, have already diagnosed President Trump as having at least a narcissistic personality disorder. Jerrold Post, political psychologist for the CIA, who has diagnosed political leaders' psyches throughout his career, has vehemently protested against the American Psychiatric Association for prohibiting psychiatrists from lending their expertise to this public discussion.

Although the American Psychiatric Association and American Psychological Association have criticized their members for violating the Goldwater rule (Benedict Carey, "The Psychiatric Question: Is It Fair to Analyze Donald Trump From Afar?" Nytimes.com, August 15, 2016), I believe the public needs the benefit of professional psychoanalytic knowledge. In the tradition of Freud, Erikson, Adorno, Sanford, Lasswell, Rangell and Bollas, psychoanalysts should be free to express their understanding of prominent political and cultural personalities of our time for the public welfare.

Recently, two dozen Congressman have called for the establishment of a commission dedicated to assessing the mental capacity of Donald Trump and have consulted a Yale psychiatrist, Dr. Bandy Lee, and three other psychiatrists as advisors. In December 2017, these professionals wrote a letter to Republican and Democratic members of Congress expressing grave concerns about President Donald Trump's psychological ability to handle the presidency, especially as the threat of nuclear war with North Korea looms over America. The letter said: "We have reason to believe that Mr. Trump's propensity for violence and war is beyond the usual of U.S presidents." "His heightened paranoia and isolation, recklessness and impulsivity, distortions of reality, rage reactions, and ever-present desire to show strength—burnishing his own sense of worth—are consistent with both an incapacity to make rational decisions and a potentially lethal proclivity to make dangerous ones."

Since this letter, Dr. Lee (2017) has published *The Dangerous Case of Donald Trump,* in which 27 psychiatrists, psychologists and other mental health professionals have diagnosed the president and concluded that he is mentally unfit to be president. Dr. Lee argued that this publication, ostensibly in violation of the Goldwater rule, is necessary because mental health professionals have a duty to warn the American public when a president poses a clear and present danger to the security of the United States.

On August 22, 2017, following President Trump's freewheeling speech in Phoenix, James Clapper, former Director of the Central Intelligence Agency under Presidents George W. Bush and Barack Obama, told CNN host Don Lemon that Trump was "downright scary and disturbing" and questioned his ability to be in office. "In a fit of pique, he decides to do something about Kim Jong Un, there's actually very little to stop him... The whole system is built to ensure rapid response if necessary. So there's very little in the way of control over exercising a nuclear option, which is pretty damn scary."

My Writing Process

$While$ writing a psychoanalytic political op-ed piece, I assume that there is a political psyche and a national psyche, and that a political administration can have its own unique psychodynamics based on the dynamics of the politicians within that administration and the voters whom they represent. My *modus operandi* includes: (1) being emotionally provoked by a current political issue that is affecting the public deeply; (2) thinking divergently about the deeper questions that need to be answered (e.g., what doesn't quite make sense); (3) discerning what psychoanalytic concepts best illuminate the unconscious psychodynamic motivations that underlie the event and enrich the public's understanding; (4) stating the controversial political question in the lead paragraph as the organizing structure of the piece; (5) considering what I know about the subject and researching it further, if necessary; and 6) discovering the implications of my political psychoanalysis, and revealing the conclusions it suggests.

When I was writing for Allison Silver, she advised me to write simply, the way I talk or think. She also cautioned me against being swayed by the politics of the event that was taking place, and neglecting the psychological dynamics, which was my area of expertise. In this kind of psychoanalytic writing, it is crucial to emphasize the unconscious psychological factors and not whatever your personal political viewpoint happens to be.

Thus, at this moment on July 22, 2017, I am provoked by the fact that under President Trump's administration, the American psyche appears to have regressed from a mature state of political cooperation between the Republican and Democratic parties during President Clinton's administration, to the uncompromising gridlock of today's congressional stalemates, what Senator John McCain has labeled "tribal politics." The symptoms of this regression: Trump's unreasonableness—his unethical, immoral behavior has shocked the liberal community and many Republicans, yet he still has enormous support from his base and the various interest groups that depend upon him. How can I psychologically explain this? What caused America's regression, and what can we do about it? While discussing this with you, I find myself actually writing the piece.

"During Clinton's administration, both parties moved toward the center, but in the ensuing years, extremists have taken over each party. For the Republicans, it has been the House Freedom Caucus, Tea Party and Christian Evangelicals. For the Democrats, it has been the Bernie Sanders socialists. Each party shuns and denigrates political compromise as weakness while intractable adherence to the party line is considered strong.

Psychoanalytically, this brings to mind the developmentally primitive defense of *splitting,* in which one thinks in terms of black and white, good and evil, etc. instead of venturing into the gray zone of mature ambivalence and compromise. Along with the predominance of splitting in congressional relations, there has been a degradation of reason, ethics and morality in the service of pursuing one's vested interests. America has regressed from reason and compromise to identity politics and tribalism, in which each group fights for its own concerns instead of thinking about the greater good for America as a whole. Each tribe privileges its narcissistic interests, so its motivation is "my vested interests, right or wrong; my family versus yours." As for President Trump, his tribe is himself. He seems to support only his own needs.

Many liberals ask, How can nearly 84% of Trump supporters, according to recent polls, still vote for him today, even though he has acted unreasonably, unethically and immorally? The answer lies in the identity politics of his voters. Most conservatives can't stand his reprehensible character and his bromance with Putin, but know he will fight for the most reactionary conservative legislation to support their business interests, smaller government, anti-immigration, and anti–climate change and and that he will nominate socially conservative justices, like

Neal Gorsuch, to the federal bench and the Supreme Court. Christian Evangelicals and Catholics find Trump morally repugnant, yet they will vote for a lying, irresponsible, unethical person because they know he will support a Christian Conservative agenda. And blue collar, white male Rust Belt workers will vote for him because of his promise to bring their jobs back, his anti-immigration policies and his strong stance against shipping their jobs overseas.

Trump supporters don't care that Trump is un-presidential, uncouth, unreasonable, and immoral or that he thinks only of his own needs. What matters is their belief that he will keep his campaign promises and try to deliver them.

The most challenging question in writing this piece is, What caused this political regression in which reason and morality no longer seem to matter? After considerable thought, I have concluded that the main cause was the enormous expansion of America's multiculturalism. As long as white Christian heterosexual male culture remained an over-whelming American majority, minorities could be tolerated to various degrees, political compromises could be reached, and reason and moral-ity could prevail. But when minority groups (Latinos, Blacks, Asians and Muslims) infiltrated so many exclusively white hamlets in American society, and with the national post-traumatic stress syndrome of 9/11 (in which foreign terrorists' attack upon America is still deeply experi-enced as a painful, open, infected wound), an insidious "whitelash" has festered. Obama's presidency was arguably the breaking point, the final straw, resoundingly ringing the death knell of white male hegemony.

With the hated specter of Hillary on the horizon, these largely white male American tribes voted for a racist, narcissistic businessman/ salesman/con man who molded his political agenda to please them. He became their authoritarian savior who said he would fix everything, and they believed him. In the movie *Being There*, Chance, the simple gardener so impressed important people, including the President of the United States, as they projected their deepest wishes onto his blank, unresponsive face (screen). Similarly, these political tribes have projected their dreams onto Trump, who promises to fulfill them. In this regressed climate of identity politics, will Trump ultimately walk on water, like Chance the Gardener, or will he sink and drown the hopes of his self-centered minions?"

As I reflect on this first draft and question how to improve it, I feel that I haven't explained enough psychoanalytically. Why was there a regression to identity politics? And how does regression to tribal politics explain the loss of reason and ethics and the ability to compromise? Also, shouldn't I include congressmen who want to work across the aisle, like Senators McCain and Schumer? Isn't it too reductionist to cite only multiculturalism as the cause of America's regression? I also want to have a fuller, more optimistic conclusion.

I have edited this piece over and over again, eliminating every excessive word, changing sentences to make them express exactly what I wanted to say. I have changed the title a number of times, and watched the word count because I knew that the maximum word count for a *Huffington Post* article was 1000, and for a *Los Angeles Times* Sunday "opinion" piece, 1200. Most newspapers like the word count for an op-ed piece to be between 500 and 750.

After completing the piece, I sent it to the *Los Angeles Times* Sunday "Opinion" section. I did this yesterday, July 29, 2017. Their submission information informed me that if I don't hear from them within three days, I am free to submit it elsewhere. My strategy is to send it to the *New York Times* "Sunday Review" next, and if they reject it, I will publish it in the *Huffington Post*. As a *Huffington Post* blogger, I can publish whatever I write without being edited. In the past, they would either accept or reject a submitted piece.

This is the piece I submitted:

America's Regressive Politics:
Its Loss of Reason, Ethics and Compromise,
A Psychoanalyst's Perspective

"Incredulous, most liberals ask, "How can nearly 84% of Trump's supporters want to vote for him today (according to recent polls) after seeing him behave so unreasonably, unethically and immorally?" I believe the answer lies in America's regression to tribal politics, as Senator John McCain so aptly put it. While many conservatives can't stand Trump's reprehensible character and his "bromance" with Putin, they believe he will fight for conservative legislation in support of their business and political interests, such as lower taxes, anti–climate change, smaller government, anti-immigration legislation, as well as appoint socially conservative justices to the Supreme Court, like Neal Gorsuch. Christian Evangelicals and Catholics find Trump morally repugnant. Yet they will vote against their religious values for an unethical, immoral person because they believe he will advance their Christian conservative agenda. And blue collar, white male Rust Belt workers will vote for him because of his promise to bring their jobs back, his anti-immigration policies and his stance against outsourcing.

In backing Trump, each tribe is identifying with its own interests and not thinking of what's best for America as a whole. The fact that Trump is egocentric, un-presidential, uncouth, unreasonable and unethical doesn't matter. What matters is their belief that he will fulfill his promises. The late Dr. Leo Rangell, President Emeritus of the International Psychoanalytical Association, in his book, *The Mind of Watergate,* called this degradation of conscience: the refusal to tell right from wrong of a president and his supporters, a "compromise of integrity."

America's political psyche has regressed from mature cooperation between the Republican and Democratic parties, especially during President Clinton's administration, to the uncompromising gridlock of today's congressional stalemate. During Clinton's era, both parties moved toward the center and passed important legislation together, but in the ensuing years, extremists have taken over each party. For the Republicans they are the House Freedom Caucus, the Tea Party and Christian Evangelicals, and for the Democrats, the Bernie Sanders' socialists and disaffected Green contingent. Each party has shunned and denigrated political compromise as "weak" while glorifying intractable adherence to the party line. Rare exceptions include Senators McCain and Schumer, who have recently exhorted party members to work across the aisle.

Unfortunately, our parties are under the regressive sway of primitive splitting, perceiving each other in terms of black and white, good and evil, "My way, or the highway." Daily, we are witnessing shocking lapses of reason, ethics and morality in today's political discourse.

Why has this regression occurred? The reasons are certainly multifold, such as the slow growth of our economy; the fear of terrorist attacks after 9/11; and the wars in Iraq, Afghanistan and Syria; but I believe that the main cause is the xenophobic reaction to the expanding multicultural complexion of American society. As long as the population remained overwhelmingly white, Christian, heterosexual and male-centric, the white majority felt secure enough to tolerate the "otherness" of minorities, to varying degrees. But when multicultural groups, such as Hispanics, Blacks, Asians and Muslims, began infiltrating so many white hamlets in America, an insidious white-lash festered that surged after 9/11. The first black President was arguably the last straw, auguring the death knell of white male hegemony.

Multiculturalism became an existential threat to white America, pre-cipitating a regression from mature political intercourse to tribal gridlock. Trump channeled the desperate wish to make America "white" again, the way it had always been. When your home is endangered, emotional loyalty to family becomes everything, to the detriment of reason and morality. It's "My family (tribe), right or wrong!" and not "Let's understand one another and work out our differences." Identity politics reigns.

After Obama's presidency and the hated vision of President Hillary Clinton on the horizon, America's white male tribes—blue collar Rust Belt workers, Republican conservatives, the Tea Party, Christian Evangelicals and the Catholic Church—voted for a misogynistic, racist, narcissistic businessman/salesman who exploitatively molded his political agenda to please them. This reminds me of Chance, the simple gardener in the movie *Being There*, who so impressed important people, including the President of the United States, as they projected their deepest wishes onto his blank, unresponsive face (screen), that they called him Chauncey, a more distinguished name. At the movie's end, we see Chance walking on water. Trump's tribal devotees projected their dreams onto him. But unlike Chance, a simple, innocent person, Trump transformed himself into an authoritarian savior who promised to fix everything they desired. Even with his low 39% approval rating and un-presidential behavior, they would vote for him today.

In this regressed political climate, will Trump ultimately walk on water, like Chance, or will he sink and drown the hopes of his true believers? Regardless of the answer, it is important to realize that the Trump administration is a regressive glitch in the long arc of American history. Multiculturalism is destined to represent the majority of Americans in the future. And as the xenophobic danger of "otherness" fades into obscurity, America's political psyche will regain its capacities for reason, ethics and compromise. The question is, when?"

When I compare both renditions of this piece, the latter one I submitted is a more complex, well-rendered, but emotionally modulated article. The first, which I wrote impulsively off the top of my head, had a bit more zest and fire. I wish I had considered that in the editing. That's the danger of editing. You can deaden your initial spontaneous outpouring of its vitality. My hope is that I didn't deaden it too much. If the *Los Angeles Times* rejects it, I will return to the older rendition and try to recapture some of its initial vitality.

I would like to say that thinking of interesting analogies, like Chance, the gardener, in the movie *Being There,* is exciting. In considering why Trump's disparate groups of voters would still support him, the notion of projecting their needs into him and exploitatively using him for their own narcissistic purposes, was beautifully represented in the projections of powerful people onto Chance. But the difference between Chance and Trump was crucial. Trump's exploitative strategy, according to his biographers Kranish and Fisher (2016), is to figure out the dreams of those he wants to influence, and then convincingly, with authoritarian panache, tell them that he can fulfill all their dreams better than anyone else. He used this strategy successfully in making business deals, and he has successfully used it in politics. Trump is a Machiavellian dream weaver.

In writing an opinion piece, I find it important to give myself the freedom to say whatever I want in the most uncensored emotional way, to put the raw clay down on paper first. Later I will have the time to use my objective discernment to sculpt and refine it. At times I love certain phrases or ideas that I use, but it is important for me not to become overly attached to them. In editing the piece, if they don't fit or if they detract from the strength of the article, I must wrestle with myself to delete them. You must be able to view your piece with a cold objective eye, as if it has an identity in its own right, completely separate from you. You then have an opportunity to transform it into what you want it to be. In effect, you become Pygmalion to your piece as Galatea. But as the artist, you need to respect the structural limitations of the subject you are writing about in order to attract the attention of newspaper and online journal editors while making it thought provoking for the lay public.

A few days ago, I learned that both the *Los Angeles Times* and the *New York Times* rejected my article. So I re-wrote it for the *Huffington Post,* including more psychological factors, and distributed it to as many people as I knew through websites and personal communication. I was amazed that the piece, now entitled "America's White-Lash and the Degradation of Reason" (page 165), anticipated the racial clashes in Charlottesville, Virginia, last weekend (April 13, 2017).

Chapter III

PSYCHOPHOBIA IN RELATION TO THE MENTALLY ILL, PSYCHOANALYSIS AND STUTTERERS

1. Eagleton and America's Psychophobia *(Los Angeles Times,* 1972)

2. A World of Psychophobia *(Los Angeles Times,* 2000)

3. Is Stuttering Biological or Psychological? A Psychoanalyst's Perspective *(Huffington Post,* 2011).

Psychophobia is endemic to the human psyche. Since I had never heard of this term before writing my first op-ed piece published in the *Los Angeles Times* in 1972, I thought I had created it. But then, partly to my chagrin and partly feeling validated, I found it in a psychological dictionary. The definition was obvious: a fear of the psychological. The public stigma and shame of having psychological problems is virtually universal. In a later piece, "A World of Psychophobia" (2000), written after becoming a psychoanalyst, I amplified the meaning to include the fear of the unconscious.

As described in the Introduction, in 1972 a journalist revealed vice-presidential nominee Senator Eagleton's history of severe depression in his youth, requiring psychiatric hospitalization and electroconvulsive treatment (ECT). The public became alarmed about his mental fitness for the office. The fear of a vice president with a mental illness went viral.

Senator Eagleton had been a highly successful politician from Missouri for many years and was so popular that the Democratic Party's presidential nominee, Governor George McGovern, had chosen him as his running mate. But these facts got lost in the nation's pandemonium about the possibility of a "crazy" in the White House. Critics accused Eagleton of lacking good judgment for not having disclosed his psychological record before McGovern nominated him.

Yet what would have happened if he had disclosed it? He wouldn't have stood a chance. I became incensed because this criticism didn't take into account the prejudice against the mentally ill without objectively considering the person's qualifications for the job. I decided to write an op-ed piece defending Eagleton's good judgment in hiding his psychological record. The piece was published on August 20, 1972.

Eagleton and America's Psychophobia

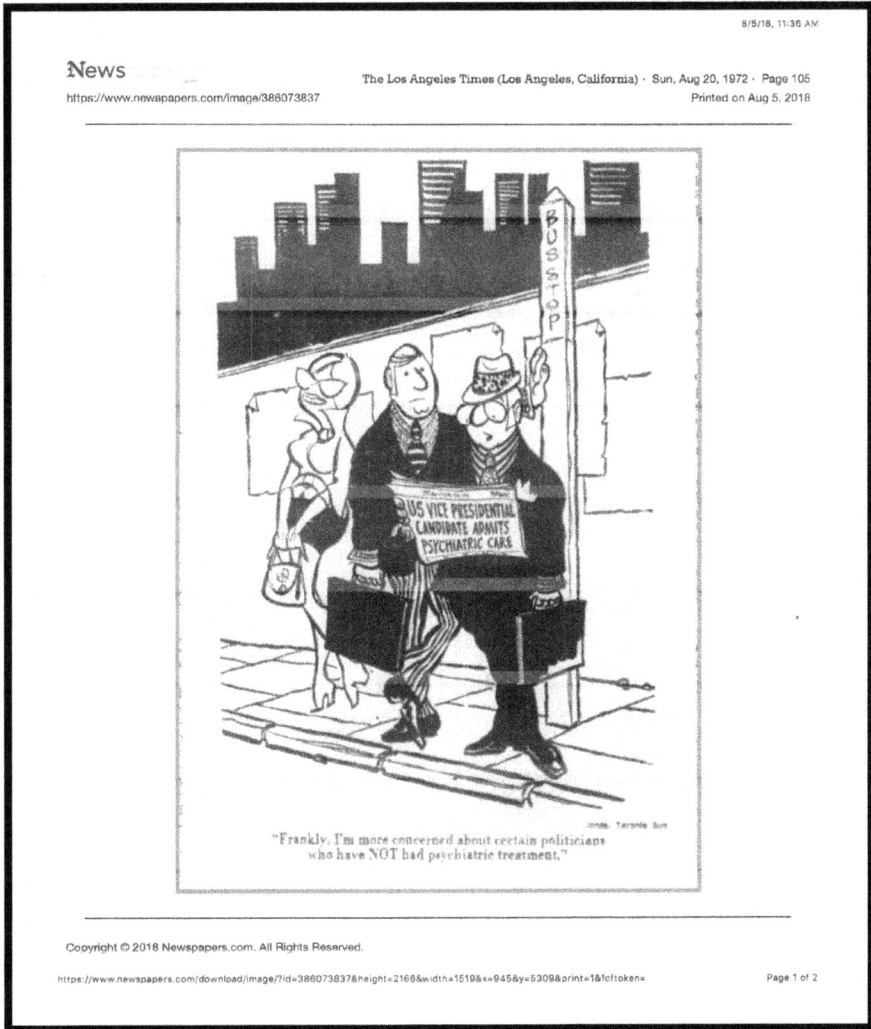

"Frankly, I'm more concerned about certain politicians who have NOT had psychiatric treatment."

"Self-styled enlightened critics of Sen. Eagleton, dismissing the mental health issue as secondary or irrelevant, urged his removal from the ticket on the basis of what they deemed as his poor judgment. When asked by George McGovern's campaign advisor, Frank Mankiewicz, about skeletons in his closet, Eagleton replied that there were none. Ergo: judgment too poor for a Vice President.

Critics contended that he should have had the common sense to realize that his psychological record was a true-blue skeleton and that it would inevitably be unearthed and would create a public furor, casting lingering doubt upon him and the McGovern candidacy.

He should have been thoroughly candid with McGovern at the outset, therefore, as a result of anticipating such negative consequences, especially if he was at all sensitive to the prospect of hurting McGovern along with himself and if he truly wanted, as he so adamantly professed, to facilitate McGovern's election.

"Eagleton was too ambitious," the critics proclaimed, and in his zealotry to fulfill his political dreams, he was blinded to the practical realities that needed to be confronted.

Continuing this analysis to its logical conclusion, good judgment would have required Eagleton to divulge his psychological problems before accepting the nomination, thereby giving McGovern and his aides a chance to consider this factor before coming to a final conclusion.

If Eagleton had done this and if McGovern's staff were as skilled at reading the political winds as their reputation affirms, they would have assessed significant elements of psychophobia—fear and repulsion of psychological problems—and dropped Eagleton from the ticket. Thus, Eagleton's "good judgment" probably would have destroyed his chances for nomination at the outset.

In this light, so-called "good judgment" would have been a totally benevolent, self-sacrificial choice, ruining Eagleton's chances for higher office for the good of the ticket and an explicit acknowledgement of the limits of his political future defined by his psychological history. He would have forsaken his personal ambitions for those of his partner and the Democratic Party.

"Good judgment," in other words, called upon him to politically martyr himself to appease the nation's psychophobia.

The principle behind this so-called good judgment is clear. Persons with a history of psychological problems and treatment, according to this principle, should be entirely candid about their record to prospective employers, even though this may evoke considerable fear, anger and discrimination, and they should courageously endure whatever adverse consequences befall them.

This is obviously a policy whereby honesty may not only not pay, but may, on the contrary, produce irremedial damage to one's career. The question is: Does good judgment dictate that one should reveal information that may be totally irrelevant to the execution of one's job and may lead to one's own detriment because of irrational prejudice?

This kind of good judgment seems to be asking "honesty" to be the innocent dupe of "discrimination" and expecting persons with psychological records to behave like martyrs.

Unlike racial discrimination, persons with psychological records can successfully hide their histories and in most cases avoid the stigma against them. In fact, many psychotherapists in the name of "good judgment" advise their patients when applying for jobs to deny their psychological problems and treatment.

Probably because such information can be so easily concealed, there has not been a large public outcry in recent history over psychological discrimination until the Eagleton affair, even though most people are covertly aware of the existence of such prejudice. Even Eagleton was apparently able to camouflage his psychological record in Missouri while running for senator.

On the basis of having weathered the storm in his home state without divulgence of his record, he probably assumed he could weather the hurricanes of a vice presidential candidacy with similar ease. Some say that this assumption also reflected poor judgment; he should have realized that many more reporters with fine-tooth combs in hand would be investigating him as vice presidential aspirant, and that he would inevitably be found out.

To know this with great certainty, however, particularly after having survived the senatorial campaign, would be nearly impossible. As it happened, one Washington reporter unfortunately closely followed up a lead that opened up Eagleton's closet.

Other critics say that concealment was justifiable in a senatorial campaign, but not in a vice presidential one, because of the significantly greater importance attached to the latter position. This appears tantamount to maintaining that the more important the job, the more one should give in to the irrational, primitive impulses of public pressure to determine one's career.

Perhaps the most crucial charge against Eagleton's withholding is that he failed to let the American people act upon the right to know the psychological condition of a candidate so that they could better evaluate whom to vote for.

This hypothetical error implicitly assumes that the American public is knowledgeable enough about psychological problems to judge the effect they will have upon performance in political office and vote accordingly. A number of enlightened critics and a few polls indicated that the majority of Americans would not have held Eagleton's psychological record against him.

However, a significant number of voters would have switched sides, and in a close presidential race similar to the last two contests, this group could make a vital difference. Obviously, many people are more likely to vote on the basis of their psychophobia than of a realistic, pragmatic appraisal.

For example, the public lack of knowledge about psychiatric hospitalization—such as the fact that many successful, energetic people have

been hospitalized for depression and have continued to perform successfully after treatment, and that electroshock therapy is so commonly used
by psychiatrists that it is employed routinely for depression on an outpatient basis—is all too apparent.

Moreover, an expert may assess that the energy, drive and intelligence
of a Sen. Eagleton may be significantly more suitable for the vice presidential slot than an individual accustomed to a slower pace who would
have to accelerate his work habits to keep up with the demands of the
office. Clearly, the public is not equipped to make a sensible judgment
concerning predictions of future performance based upon a psychological treatment record.

Eagleton did what most persons with a history of psychological problems, good judgment and a normal sense of self-preservation should do
under similar circumstances—that is, conceal their record of treatment
when a question of employment is at stake in order to protect themselves
against psychological discrimination. Unfortunately, he got caught.

One salutary feature of his experience, however, is that psychological
discrimination has been revealed as a deep-seated, insidious national
problem requiring an organized psychological liberation movement to
combat it. But who will volunteer?

Naturally, if everyone were honest about treatment records when
seeking employment, there would be many more cases of obvious discrimination and a great felt need for such a movement, but who is willing to be the sacrificial lamb when psychological problems are usually so
easy to hide. Should Sen. Eagleton have been?"

Commentary: Most of the *Times'* letters to the editor were supportive of my viewpoint, especially organizations championing the rights of
the mentally ill.

Having received my Ph.D. in clinical psychology from Southern Illinois
University after completing my internship at Mount Zion Hospital in
San Francisco in 1968 and my postdoctoral fellowship at Colorado

Psychiatric Hospital in Denver in 1969, I was extremely sensitized to the human fear of having psychological problems and the reluctance of patients to reveal and explore them in psychotherapy. Between 1970 and 1977, in private practice in Beverly Hills, California, I employed a number of therapeutic modalities, such as psychodrama, Gestalt therapy, marathon therapy, desensitization, counterconditioning, implosive therapy, hypnosis, transactional analysis and psychodynamic therapy, to facilitate therapeutic awareness and cathartic abreactions. Identifying with my academic training as a clinical psychologist—a scientist-practitioner model—I subscribed to an experimental ideology of clinical intervention based on the underlying assumption that psychotherapy was a pioneering venture with little definitive knowledge. Consequently, psychologists needed to choose from the vast array of therapeutic modalities, those that worked best for different types of patients. When I told a distinguished psychoanalyst how I was practicing, he said, "Pete, it sounds like you're making stew." I knew he was right, and realized that I was acting omnipotently, trying to select and integrate qualitatively diverse theories and techniques of psychotherapy into a seamless therapeutic amalgam. I began to envy some friends who had recently become candidates at the Los Angeles Institute and Society for Psychoanalytic Studies, which was founded by psychologists, clinical social workers and psychiatrists, and adopted the rigorous tripartite model of the International Psychoanalytical Association. To reduce my envy, I became a candidate for psychoanalytic training at this institute.

When I began this training in 1977, I realized that the therapeutic modalities I used were essentially superficial, manipulative techniques that lacked a comprehensive theory of the human mind and its development. At best, they produced short-term results for patients with superficial problems, but failed to treat the majority of cases requiring long-term psychotherapy. I became aware that psychoanalysis was the only form of psychotherapy that had a comprehensive theory of development, unconscious motivation and working in the transference. I knew that if I wanted to become the best psychotherapist I could be, I had to become a psychoanalyst.

It wasn't until I received psychoanalytic training in the late 70s and early 80s that I realized that psychophobia had a more profound meaning than a fear of the psychological. Its deepest meaning was a fear of unconscious impulses, thoughts, perceptions and feelings. As a psychoanalyst, I became acutely aware of the universal human resistance against exploring the unconscious because this evoked the greatest shame and guilt about forbidden sexual and aggressive impulses and about one's most vulnerable feelings, thoughts and desires. In other words, psychoanalysis itself threatened to evoke the greatest psychophobia. Consequently, it was understandable that most patients would prefer short-term directive behavioral treatment with no extensive exploration of one's mind or past.

I identified with this fear of psychoanalysis easily, especially since my graduate school at Southern Illinois University denigrated it as archaic and ineffectual compared with behavior therapy, rational emotive therapy, Gestalt therapy, etc. Until my psychoanalytic internship at Mount Zion Hospital, I didn't realize that my identification with academic psychology's prejudice against psychoanalysis had turned me against the source of my original attraction to psychology. I had unconsciously become a victim of a kind of Stockholm syndrome, or as Anna Freud would put it, identification with the aggressor, against what had inspired me to become a psychologist in the first place. This prejudice against psychoanalysis was reinforced by the fact that psychoanalysis was dominated by psychiatry in America, a medical profession that excluded psychologists and other non-medical mental health professionals from practicing it. To obtain psychoanalytic training at one of the medical psychoanalytic institutes, I would have had to sign a waiver agreeing that I would only perform psychoanalytic research and not practice psychoanalysis.

In 1987, as a result of a lawsuit promulgated by the American Psychological Association against the American Psychoanalytic

Association and the International Psychoanalytical Association, the medical monopoly over psychoanalysis in the United States ended. Non-medical institutes with equivalent standards, like my own (LAISPS), were now evaluated for admission into the International Psychoanalytical Association (IPA), which Freud had established in 1910 to maintain the highest standards of psychoanalytic training, research and practice. Carl Jung was its first president.

In contrast, the vast majority of clinical psychology programs in the United States devalued psychoanalysis as an archaic, outmoded theory and treatment. Consequently, there were exceptionally few psychoanalytically-oriented undergraduate and graduate psychology programs. And this remains true today. Ironically, the medical field of psychiatry has shifted from psychoanalysis to psychopharmacology and has jumped on the academic psychology bandwagon of embracing cognitive behavior therapy. Psychology's and psychiatry's prejudice against psychoanalysis is a glaring symptom of psychophobia, and this prejudice reinforces the public's fear of exploring one's deepest unconscious conflicts and psychological deficits. As a psychoanalyst, I realized that psychophobia was not only a fear of the psychological, but also a fear of the unconscious.

On May 28, 2000, the *Los Angeles Times* published my second piece on psychophobia, the piece I had sent to Otto Kernberg. If you recall, this was in response to a travelling Freud exhibit that had arrived at the Skirball Cultural Center in Los Angeles and had provoked an onslaught of Freud-bashing, especially by Frederick Crews, professor emeritus of English at the University of California at Berkeley and a notorious Freud hater. His screeds against psychoanalysis were frequently published in the *New York Review of Books*.

In this piece, I tried to explain why psychoanalysis has always gener-ated antipathy, even when Freud first introduced it to the medical society in Vienna.

A World of Psychophobia

COMMENTARY / ANALYSIS / TIMES INTERVIEW

SECTION

M

OPINION

SUNDAY
MAY 28, 2000

A World of Psychophobia

PERSONAL PERSPECTIVE

By Peter Wolson

Sigmund Freud's pioneering discoveries about mankind's psyche have fascinated the public for more than a century, yet they have consistently provoked harsh criticism. The current controversy over Freud and psychoanalysis, precipitated by the Freud exhibit at the Skirball Cultural Center, is but the latest round in a long series of critiques of Freud. In fact, anti-Freudian attitudes almost scuttled this exhibit when it was first mounted at the Smithsonian in Washington. These attacks against psychoanalysis often extend beyond scientific criticism and appear to be a symptom of America's psychophobia: the fear of what lurks psychologically in the unconscious mind.

Since Freud began his work, humanity has sought to deny the power of its unconscious and displayed an aversion to examining it. In fact, psychophobia is ubiquitous in human nature and has prompted defensive assaults on psychoanalysis from its inception.

But just what is so threatening about Freud's idea that human behavior is motivated by unconscious psychological forces?

Certainly, Freud offended mankind's hubris. Human beings generally believe they should be able to control their lives through conscious willpower, and Freud's theory that they are motivated by unconscious psychodynamics threatens their sense of personal control. It leaves people feeling somewhat helpless, less certain about navigating their lives. Freud then added insult to injury by portraying human beings as motivated by sexual and aggressive animalistic impulses. This was a shattering blow to the belief of human superiority over animals.

But perhaps the greatest threat of Freudian theory concerned what lurks in the unconscious mind. Many people are afraid of their dark side. They fear if they examine their deepest emotional recesses, especially in the presence of an analyst, they will uncover what is worst about themselves and feel unbearable shame or guilt. For example, it is not uncommon for people to suspect they are crazy and that psychoanalysis will validate this. Other fears include being too aggressive, exhibitionistic, perverted, selfish, dependent or depressed. The anticipation of uncovering these undesirable traits and impulses can threaten one's psychic survival.

Moreover, many experience the prospect of psychoanalysis as endangering vital ties to loved ones. For example, psychoanalytic patients often resist remembering their childhood because they fear they will end up blaming their parents for their problems and feel guilty for betraying them. Such patients often insist therapy has nothing to do with exploring the past and reject Freudian therapy.

Wake-up call: Sigmund Freud in 1921.

Library of Congress

loved ones, and how one's defense against knowing about it contributes to psychological symptoms. Because psychophobia is so endemic to human nature, the process of psychoanalysis involves a continual exploration of the patient's resistance to knowing what is dreaded in the unconscious mind.

It is, therefore, not surprising that most Americans would prefer to have a physical illness, for which there is a remedy like ones as suggested by the prevalence of psychosomatic ailments: physical symptoms—for example, stomach aches—caused by an emotional problem. It has been estimated that more than 50% of a physician's practice involves the treatment of psychosomatic complaints.

Even medical schools seem to have submitted to psychophobia by training psychiatrists almost exclusively as psychopharmacologists instead of as psychotherapists.

Perhaps the most deleterious influence of America's psychophobia has been on the managed-care system, in which mental illness has received significantly less credibility and financial support than physical illness under the rationale of saving money. Thus, insurance companies have been found to cover physical illness over mental illness by a ratio of seven to one, though studies have demonstrated that psychotherapy significantly reduces the frequency of physical complaints.

Ironically, even with managed care's psychophobic slide toward discriminatory reimbursement of psychopharmacologists and behavior therapists, mental-health professionals seem to regard psychoanalysis as the most interesting game in town. This is because classical Freudian theory provides the most comprehensive understanding of the complexity of human psychological functioning. The psychoanalytic training institutes in Los Angeles have more than doubled in recent years, to accommodate this growing interest.

Freud's greatness was attributable to the fact that "he disturbed people's sleep"

"Sigmund Freud's discoveries about mankind's psyche have fascinated the public for more than a century, yet they have consistently provoked harsh criticism. The current controversy of Freud and psychoanalysis, precipitated by the Freud exhibit at the Skirball Cultural Center, is but the latest round in a long series of criticisms of Freud. In fact, anti-Freudian attitudes almost scuttled this exhibit when it was first mounted at the Smithsonian in Washington, DC. These attacks against psychoanalysis often extend beyond scientific criticism and appear to be a symptom of America's psychophobia: the fear of what lurks psychologically in the unconscious mind.

Since Freud began his work, humanity has sought to deny the power of its unconscious and displayed an aversion to examining it. In fact, psychophobia is ubiquitous in human nature and has prompted defensive assaults against psychoanalysis from its inception.

But just what is so threatening about Freud's idea that human behavior is motivated by unconscious psychological forces?

Certainly, Freud offended mankind's hubris. Human beings generally believe they should be able to control their lives through conscious willpower, and Freud's theory that they are motivated by unconscious psychodynamics threatens their sense of personal control. It leaves people feeling somewhat helpless, less certain about navigating their lives. Freud then added insult to injury by portraying human beings as motivated by their sexual and aggressive animalistic impulses. This was a shattering blow to the belief of human superiority over other animals.

But perhaps the greatest threat of Freudian theory concerned what lurks in the unconscious mind. Many people are afraid of their dark side. They fear if they examine their deepest emotional recesses, especially in the presence of an analyst, they will uncover what is worst about themselves and feel unbearable shame or guilt. For example, it is not uncommon for people to suspect they are crazy and that psychoanalysis will validate this. Other fears include being too aggressive, exhibitionistic, perverted, selfish, dependent or depressed. The anticipation of uncovering these undesirable traits and impulses can threaten one's psychic survival.

Moreover, many experience the prospect of psychoanalysis as endangering their vital ties to loved ones. For example, psychoanalytic patients often resist remembering their childhood because they fear they will end up blaming their parents for their problems and feel guilty for betraying them. Such patients often insist therapy has nothing to do with exploring the past and reject Freudian therapy.

Yet the Freudian analyst would help the patient become aware of the psychological danger of uncovering and understanding the basis of animosity toward loved ones, and how one's defense against knowing about it contributes to psychological symptoms. Because psychophobia is so endemic to human nature, the process of psychoanalysis involves a continuous exploration of the resistance to understanding what is dreaded in the unconscious mind.

It is therefore not surprising that most Americans would prefer to have a physical illness, for which there is a remedy, like medication or surgery, than a psychological disturbance calling for psychoanalysis. Even the "unconscious" frequently prefers physical problem to psychological ones, as suggested by the prevalence of psychosomatic ailments: physical symptoms—for example, stomach aches—caused by an emotional problem. It has been estimated that more than 50% of a physician's practice involves the treatment of psychosomatic complaints.

Even medical schools seem to have submitted to psychophobia by training psychiatrists almost exclusively as psychopharmacologists instead of as psychotherapists.

Perhaps the most deleterious influence of America's psychophobia has been on the managed care system, in which mental illness has received significantly less credibility and financial support than physical illness under the rationale of saving money. Thus, insurance companies have been found to cover physical illness over mental illness by a ratio of seven to one, though studies have demonstrated that psychotherapy significantly reduces the frequency of physical complaints.

Ironically, even with managed care's psychophobic slide toward discriminatory reimbursement of psychopharmacologists and behavior therapists, mental health professionals seem to regard psychoanalysis as the most interesting game in town. This is because classical Freudian theory provides the most comprehensive understanding of human psychological functioning. The psychoanalytic institutes in Los Angeles have more than doubled in recent years to accommodate this growing interest.

Freud's greatness was attributable to the fact that he "disturbed people's sleep" by making them aware of their deepest feelings and thoughts. We need to watch out for our psychophobic inclination to take a pill and go back to sleep."

This op-ed piece received a huge positive response from the Los Angeles psychoanalytic community. Some internship and postdoctoral psychology instructors began assigning this article to their psychotherapy students, to acquaint them with various types of unconscious resistance to psychoanalytic exploration.

The last piece I wrote on psychophobia was similar to the Eagleton one in its emphasis on the public stigma of psychological problems. This piece is about stuttering. The movie *The King's Speech* motivated me to write it. It was about "Bertie," who reluctantly became King George VI of England when his brother, King Edward VIII (later known as the Duke of Windsor), abdicated the throne to marry Wally Simpson, an American divorcee. The movie brilliantly showed how Bertie overcame his stuttering by expressing anger at his speech therapist, Lionel Logue (who in real life was psychoanalytically oriented), who represented his father in the transference. This illustrated how overcoming repressed rage toward his dominating father reduced Bertie's symptom of stuttering. This suggested that Bertie's internal psychological conflict over his aggression toward his father was a major cause of his stuttering.

In researching this issue, I was shocked to learn that the two major national associations dedicated to stutterers and the treatment of stuttering proclaimed that the cause of stuttering was completely biological. As a former stutterer, I vehemently disagreed. As a young child of divorced parents, when I lived with one parent, my stuttering increased, but then virtually disappeared when I lived with the other parent. The psychological atmosphere of my childhood environment was so obviously the cause of my stuttering that this strongly influenced my choice to become a psychologist. During my analysis, I came to realize that my stuttering was related to inhibited rage. While stuttering, I unconsciously attacked my own speech for fear and guilt over expressing anger toward loved ones who would not want to hear what I had to say, and I unconsciously feared they would retaliate and abandon me.

Although I did not write this in the blog, I suspect that the motivation of the national stuttering associations to make its cause completely biological was psychophobia, trying to avoid the stigma and shame associated with psychological causation.

On December 16, 2011, the following article was published in the *Huffington Post*.

Is Stuttering Biological or Psychological?

"The Stuttering Foundation of America has proclaimed on its website (www.stutteringhelp.org), "There is no reason to believe that emotional trauma causes stuttering." Similarly, the National Stuttering Association (www.nsastutter.org) has stated, "We do know that stuttering is not caused by emotional problems and is not a nervous disorder. We also know that stuttering is not the fault of the family or the person who stutters."

These organizations suggest that stuttering is primarily an inherited disorder unrelated to environmental upbringing. Based on case studies, I, a psychoanalyst, am convinced that the exclusive emphasis on biological cause is misguided insofar as it rules out psychoanalytic therapy for those stutterers whose speech disorder derives from internal conflicts due to family influences, as was strikingly evident in last year's academy award winning film, *The King's Speech*. This film was based on historical fact.

From its viewpoint, Bertie, who became King George VI, was portrayed as intimidated and frightened by his oppressive father, the King of England, during childhood. The film implied that this caused him to become fearful of expressing himself verbally, especially his anger. From a psychoanalytic perspective, the expression of his own speech apparently represented transgressing against his father. Bertie's symptom of stuttering served the defensive function of blocking any provocative speech, while making him look inadequate, thereby diminishing the fear of his aggression and its anxiety-inducing consequences.

Although his Australian speech therapist Lionel Logue treated him with various speech exercises, what appeared to help most was when he provoked Bertie's anger, first by having him say the "F word" over and over again, and then by acting like a dominating father figure while sitting on the king's royal throne. Enraged, Bertie screamed at Logue and was amazed when Logue pointed out that he wasn't stuttering. In effect, the stuttering diminished when he was able to express his anger. The speech therapist's friendship and his support of Bertie's right to express his own independent feelings and thoughts, especially his anger, and especially when the therapist represented a dominating father figure, ultimately made Bertie feel safe enough to speak freely. This is what happens in psychoanalysis when the patient might experience the therapist in the transference as, for example, a repressive parental figure. The therapist then helps the patient work through his fear of expressing aggression toward dominating father figures in the transference relationship.

In various interviews, the writer-producer of *The King's Speech*, David Seidler, a stutterer himself, speculated that in real life, Bertie benefitted most from his speech therapist's "talking cure" based on Freudian psychoanalysis, not from the mechanical speech exercises portrayed in the film. In fact, Seidler said that most of the speech therapists he consulted agreed that speech exercises, while helpful to some extent, didn't eliminate stuttering. He concluded that Logue must have used Freud's "talking cure" based on the fact that Seidler's uncle, who was also a stutterer, had been coincidentally, treated by Lionel Logue for years. His uncle said that Logue got him to talk about his parents and childhood, and although his uncle considered all of that rubbish, by the time his treatment ended, he no longer stuttered (www.dailymail.co.uk).

Seidler noted that he wished he had someone like Logue to have listened to him attentively and helped him understand his life better. Bertie, in *The King's Speech*, clearly didn't grow up with a father or brother who were lovingly attuned and supportive of him. But Lionel Logue, his speech therapist, helped him to repair these experiential deficits and to resolve his internal psychological conflict over his aggression.

Similarly, Jack Welch, former CEO of General Electric, on June 11, 2011, confided to TV guest host Piers Morgan, that he was a stutterer. He said that what helped him most was his mother's belief in the value of what he had to say and her encouragement to speak his mind. He felt listened to and understood by her, and she supplied her reassuring explanation that his intelligent mind worked more rapidly than his capacity to speak his ideas. In effect, she validated his right to say what he wanted and to be his authentic self.

There is abundant research evidence for a biological predisposition for stuttering; however, environmental stressors, such as family relations, can produce internal psychological conflicts that cause stuttering, possibly in combination with this biological predisposition, as in the case history cited above, and in the psychodynamics of King George VI depicted in the film *The King's Speech*. That is why I urge stutterers and organizations devoted to the treatment of stuttering to consider psychoanalytic therapy as an often essential part of the treatment for this debilitating, humiliating psychological symptom. Proclaiming that stuttering is unrelated to family relationships and emotional issues is a misguided, potentially damaging omission for individuals whose stuttering is largely caused by psychological conflicts in childhood."

Commentary: This piece was highly controversial, with many comments attacking me and defending the position of the stuttering associations, but many others agreed with me. TV medical pundit, Dr. Oz, quoted this article as a contemporary perspective on the etiology of stuttering (February 8, 2013; (http://blog.doctoroz.com/you-wanted-to-know/why-do-people-stutter).

The position taken by the National Stuttering Association in reassuring stutterers that the symptoms of stuttering have nothing to do with emotional problems caused by family experiences in childhood was a poorly disguised, politically correct attempt to avoid the shame and guilt associated with exploring psychological factors. Most people assume incorrectly that if you have a psychological problem, you have lacked the willpower and strength of character to overcome it. This implies, in effect, that you have chosen it. On the other hand, if they know the problem is biologically caused, they blame you less because you did not choose to have the problem. You inherited it and therefore couldn't help it.

One can see this same form of denial operating in defining alcoholism as a medical disease instead of a psychological problem. Having a physical illness is excusable because you can't help it, whereas a psychological malady is seen as an indication of weakness, as if you had chosen to become an alcoholic because of your weak character. This ignorant belief doesn't consider the fact that environmental causes of psychological problems are just as determined as biological ones. One does not choose one's neuroses, character disorders or psychoses. Sigmund Freud established this conclusively with his concept of psychological determinism. Every psychological problem is developmentally caused. So many of our psychotherapy patients have trouble accepting this, and feel guilty about blaming their parents. Instead, under the influence of psychophobia, they feel mortifying shame and blame themselves harshly for being in therapy and continuing to struggle with their symptoms, as if they had a choice in the matter. Thus, all psychological problems are unconsciously determined developmentally and biologically, with different loadings of each causative factor, depending on the type of problem.

But even when there is a heavy biological loading, as in the case of Senator Eagleton's Bipolar II disorder (1972), or in some cases of stuttering or fetal alcohol syndrome, the public stigma prevails. We constantly have to battle against a "world of psychophobia," against the fear, shame and guilt concerning what lurks in the human unconscious.

Chapter IV

THE INFLUENCE OF PSYCHOLOGICAL DEVELOPMENT ON PRESIDENTIAL LEADERSHIP

1. When Politics Is Also Psychology *(Los Angeles Times,* 1999)
2. The Bush Boys: No Sibling rivalry, but Maybe Something Deeper *(Thomson Reuters,* 2015)

During the presidential campaigns of Al Gore and George W. Bush in 1999, Allison Silver asked me to write a piece comparing the influence of fathering on the leadership potential of these candidates. After considerable research based upon biographies of Gore and Bush and numerous frustrating rewrites, with Allison at one point asking if I was ready to let it go, she accepted the article. The piece was published in the *Los Angeles Times* on December 5, 1999.

When Politics Is Also Psychology

LOS ANGELES TIMES   SUNDAY, DECEMBER 5, 1999

COMMENTARY / ANALYSIS / TIMES INTERVIEW

When Politics Is Also Psychology

STEVE McAFEE / For The Times

THE NATION

By Peter Wolson

The father-son dynamic is an essential human relationship. Fathers wield powerful influences on their sons into adulthood, even when their children emerge as accomplished men in their own right, like Vice President Al

It is natural for a son to turn to his father as an ideal model of how to feel, think and act like a male. To facilitate masculine- and self-consolidation, a father needs to accept his son's idealization and help the boy realize he can grow up and embody the paternal qualities he prizes, such as physical strength or intellect. This process strengthens the son's self-

"The father–son dynamic is an essential human relationship. Fathers wield powerful influences on sons into adulthood, even when children emerge as accomplished men in their own right, like Vice President Gore and Texas Gov. George W. Bush.

When examining this key relationship, it could well be that the leading presidential contenders of both the Republican and the Democratic parties are pursuing the nomination, in part, to please their fathers. In a recent *New Yorker* article, President Bill Clinton is reported to have said that the only reason Gore ever sought the presidency was to please his father. Florida Gov. Jeb Bush is quoted in a recent biography of his older brother to the effect that George W. has felt pressure of living up to his father's example all his life.

Psychologically, why are fathers important to sons?

It is natural for a son to turn to father as an ideal model of how to feel, think and act like a male. To facilitate masculine- and self-consolidation, a father needs to accept his son's idealization and help the boy realize he can grow up and embody the paternal qualities he prizes such as physical strength or intellect. This process strengthens the son's self-confidence and sense of direction. When the father is extraordinary or inaccessible, or a combination of both, the son's idealization can increase monumentally. This makes it harder to believe he can ever fill his father's shoes.

Both Gore and Bush had powerful, successful but largely absent fathers according to their respective biographers, Bob Zelnick and Bill Minutaglio. Brothers Jeb and George W. referred to their father as a "beacon." George W. believed his father was superior to most men at whatever he did. The son's academic and work history virtually replicated his father's, but, in many instances, the son fell short of his father's accomplishments. His underachievement could well have been a reaction to the pressure he experienced trying to live up to his father's image.

By providing mentoring and guidance, fathers help their sons acquire masculine backbone by learning self-discipline, responsibility and self-reliance. But sons also need support for their autonomy, their entitlement to do things their own way. When a father dominates and uses his son as a self-extension, the son is likely to have difficulty discovering exactly who he is.

For example, Gore's father, Tennessee Sen. Al Gore Sr., might have been too domineering, according to Zelnick's biography of the vice president. The senior Gore expected "obedience and good results on the farm, in school and at home, but [was] slow to offer praise when his son performed, simply issuing a new set of tasks." Apparently, Gore Jr. became so intent on being good that Eleanor Smotherman, his second-grade teacher said, "Al Gore Jr. was so mature and advanced that I had to almost look at him to see if he was a child or a man."

While Gore Sr.'s attitude might have contributed to his son's self-discipline, was Gore Jr. able to sufficiently free himself from his father's control to attain his own identity? Could the need to please his dominating father partly account for his "woodenness"? Could this same dynamic have been operating while he served as vice president to Clinton, a political-father representative, according to close associates? Certainly, Gore is now searching, quite openly, for a separate and winning political persona.

Similarly, Minutaglio reports that George W. Bush was intimidated by his father's disapproval. Barbara Bush explained her husband's disciplinary method: "The way George scolded was by silence or by saying, 'I'm disappointed in you: And they [his sons] would almost faint." "He would be made to feel that he had committed the worst crime in history," is the way his younger brother, Marvin Bush, described George W. Bush's reaction to their father. When 19-year-old George W. quit working on an inland barge seven days before his job commitment was to end, his father said, "I just want you to know that you have disappointed me." George W. ran out of his office and has said he remembered those words for years. Is the son still intimidated by his awesome internalized father?

In addition to idealizing, every boy needs to be able to compete with and de-idealize his father to individuate. Developmentally, this normally takes place during the Oedipal phase and adolescence. The Oedipal period occurs between the age of 3 and 6, when little boys unconsciously compete with fathers for their mothers' love. The outcome of this competition will ultimately determine the individual's capacity to assert himself and take initiative without guilt, humiliation or fear of retaliation.

If the boy has not resolved his Oedipal competition, he might remain stuck in the psychological mode of pleasing father. Then, asserting himself and taking initiative could induce humiliating comparisons between himself and his "larger than life" father, resulting in unbearable feelings of inadequacy. Or such independent initiative could provoke debilitating guilt for competitively "attacking" the father.

Bush, for example, expressed Oedipal anxiety during his father's 1988 presidential campaign, according to Minutaglio, when he commented it would be better for him if his father lost the election and retired to private life because of the enormous expectations for a son in politics whose father was president. However, he now appears to be comfortable with the support of his father. But to what degree? Is George W. still fearful of competing with his internalized father, and has he fully differentiated and become his own man?

A son's ultimate individuation is achieved through what is commonly called adolescent "rebellion," the prelude to adult independence. In growing up, the adolescent challenges his father's values, often somewhat self-destructively. Such self-destructive oppositionality tends to prove father right, thereby expressing an unconscious, regressive longing to remain a child. After achieving sufficient independence, a son can risk valuing his father again, without being threatened by his regressive wishes. As Mark Twain wryly noted, "When I was 14, my father was so ignorant I could hardly stand to have the old man around. But when I got to be 21, I was astonished at how much he had learned in seven years."

If an adult has not experienced a normal adolescent rebellion, he could be self-destructively prone to defying authority figures. For example, it is unclear to what extent Gore Jr. was ever able to rebel against his father. Currently, he is defying Clinton by rejecting his help. Moreover, Gore is apparently unwilling to emphasize his own contributions to the achievements of the man whom he recently considered one of "America's best presidents." Gore has declared his intention to stop functioning as vice president to pursue his personal ambition of the presidency. Yet, this oppositionality could backfire politically, if he appears to shirk his current responsibilities.

Clearly, fathers can have a powerful, enduring influence on the psychological functioning of their adult sons. It remains to be seen whether George W. is more than an animated, personable reflection of his idealized moderate Republican father or whether Gore can find his natural political identity—some comfortable middle ground between placating and rebelling against his internalized father—before alienating the voting public. The coming campaign might hinge on which of these sons is more capable of transcending the name of the father and speaking with his own voice."

Commentary: In this piece, I was able to explore numerous psychodynamics in father–son relationships. These include the developmental importance of the experience of idealization for a son in helping to develop and strengthen his self ideal. One's ego ideal helps a person forge a sense of direction and life goals. So many patients who have lacked this normative experience appear to be lost, without purpose or meaningful objectives. As a result of this developmental deficit, they frequently manifest idealizing transferences with their analyst, not as a defense against aggression, as some Kleinians might argue, but as a developmental arrest that needs repair, from a Kohutian perspective. The treatment of this deficit involves the analyst's acceptance of the idealization, implicitly and at times explicitly communicating a belief in the patient's capacity to become like his idealized analyst-father and/or analyst-mother.

However, when one's father is exceptionally accomplished and does not actively support the son's efforts to be like him or like himself, the son can end up feeling that his goals are impossible dreams, and react with futility and hopelessness about pursuing them. In the case of Bush, this dynamic seemed to interact with Oedipal rivalry when, in his early twenties, he arrived home drunk one day and challenged his father to a fist fight (Minutaglio, 1999). His father avoided the confrontation.

If, on the other hand, a son's paternal ideal is too dominating, with the son serving, in effect, as a narcissistic extension, the son would probably have difficulty differentiating himself and finding his own voice, as arguably happened with Al Gore. When Gore tried to differentiate himself from Clinton in what appeared to be a belated adolescent rebellion against Clinton as possibly a father representative, he "threw the baby out with the bath water" by rejecting everything having to do with Clinton. Like the oppositional adolescent, in his presidential campaign against George W., he rejected Clinton's support and refused to take credit for his substantial accomplishments as Clinton's vice president. Only when adolescents achieve a more separate identity can they have the freedom to agree with their fathers without perceiving their agreement as a humiliating submission, but as their own independent choice.

George W. Bush was more successful in differentiating from his father than was Al Gore during the election campaign, and Bush won the election. But at the start of his presidential administration, Bush had trouble representing himself as a strong, independent leader. To compensate for this, he went so far as to call himself "the decider," to combat the media and public suspicion that he was a puppet of Vice President Dick Cheney. In hindsight, compared with Donald Trump's ill-suited presidency, George W. is currently looking quite presidential, even to many liberals who had loathed him.

In contrast, Al Gore, while having lost the presidency, uniquely distinguished himself as a leader of climate change, for which he won the Nobel Peace Prize in 2007. His Oscar-winning film, *An Inconvenient Truth,* was widely acclaimed. He recently released a second film on climate change, aptly titled *An Inconvenient Sequel: Truth to Power.*

I again addressed the issue of separation—individuation in a piece published by *Thomson Reuters* in 2015. Allison Silver, now as chief editor of *Thomson Reuters'* blog section, asked me to write an article on how the sibling rivalry between Jeb Bush, a contender for the Republican presidential nomination, and his older brother, former President George W. Bush, was affecting Jeb's campaign. She wondered if sibling rivalry might have contributed to his difficulty responding when reporters asked him if, knowing what he knew now (namely, that Saddam Hussein was not developing a nuclear weapon), would he have responded differently than his brother did (invading Iraq). After thinking about this, I concluded that the main psychodynamic was probably not sibling rivalry, as many journalists had speculated, but possibly Jeb's difficulty individuating from his family. This piece was published on May 21, 2015.

The Bush Boys: No Sibling Rivalry, but Maybe Something Deeper

"When Jeb Bush launched his exploratory campaign for the 2016 Republican presidential nomination earlier this year, he declared, *"I am my own man."* The former Florida governor said he was very different from both his father, President George H. W. Bush, and his older brother, President George W. Bush—though he made a point of adding, "I love my father and my brother."

Last week, however, Jeb Bush undermined his declaration of independence when he took four days to answer a question: Would he have invaded Iraq, as did his brother, knowing what we know now? In answering, Bush seemed to mishear the question, since he appeared more focused on what he wanted to tell his family than on what he wanted to tell the American public.

"Yes," he declared, he would have invaded Iraq based on the intelligence information at the time—and so would have Hillary Clinton. Over the week, it took Bush three more tries, with three different excuses, to clarify this and say "No".

Bush's answer was puzzling and unsettling to many voters because a large majority of Americans now view the war in Iraq as a serious blunder. He seemed reluctant to disagree with his older brother. This triggered widespread armchair (psychological) speculation about whether he was capable of clearly seeing events beyond the "filter" of his brother.

Many political analysts wondered if Bush's confusing responses were due to sibling rivalry. But it sounds more likely that he has difficulty separating from his family. Something has made it hard for him to have his own voice.

Though Bush, and the entire Bush family, regularly dismiss analysis of family dynamics as "psychobabble," an examination could prove helpful. There is relatively little evidence of sibling rivalry in Bush's convoluted series of answers to the question about going to war in Iraq. If it had played a significant part in his self-destructive political alignment with his older brother, we would probably have seen indications of hostility toward his brother. That is not the case.

Nonetheless, one can still hypothesize that if there had been unconscious sibling rivalry, Bush would have avoided expressing any aggressive, competitive feelings and masked any hostility. Instead, he would have strongly agreed with the invasion. But without any suggestion of recent dissension between the brothers, this is a highly speculative stretch.

Other aspects of sibling rivalry are also absent. True, Jeb once bragged he was a better reader than his older brother George. But this is scant evidence for deep sibling rivalry. The brothers also are reportedly emotionally distant because they have little social interaction and don't regularly confide in each other.

One reason so many political analysts cite sibling rivalry to be at work, however, is that Jeb Bush was the brother long viewed as presidential material, which Bush family members have acknowledged. Though George was seven years older, he was usually described as less serious and more impulsive. He was often considered the political enforcer when his father was president; his younger brother advised on policy. But when George won the Texas governorship, and Jeb lost his first gubernatorial race in Florida that same year, the family tide reputedly turned toward supporting George for the presidency. Since then, Jeb has largely existed in his brother's shadow.

New York Times op-ed columnist Maureen Dowd, for one, has helped bolster the sibling-rivalry theory. She wrote on Sunday that Jeb has "voluntarily shackled himself to W." But this seemed clear to her in 1993, when she interviewed Jeb during his first run for Florida governor. "He seemed mildly annoyed," Dowd wrote, "that his raffish older brother had jumped into the arena to run for governor in Texas. W. was co-opting Jeb's campaign lines and making it ... 'a *People* magazine story'..."

But if sibling rivalry is unlikely, there is convincing evidence of Jeb's internal conflict between his desire to become "his own man" and his fear of separating from and antagonizing his family, especially the brother he idealized as a child. This dynamic may be even more conflicted because Jeb's personal history demonstrates that he has already strongly differentiated himself from his family to become his own man.

He married a Mexican woman whose father had been a waiter and migrant worker, not a society debutant. He became fluent in Spanish and converted to Catholicism. His policies as Florida governor were far closer to conservative than moderate. He also made Florida his home rather than the family favorites, Maine and Texas.

Separating from your family is part of growing up. You go from extreme dependency as a baby and throughout childhood to the independence of adulthood. Teenage acts of rebellion, when adolescents can disagree with virtually everything parents say and stand for—is part of this transition. The turbulence of adolescence reflects the internal conflict between a teen's desire to remain a child and the desire to separate and become his or her own person. It culminates in a break that enables teenagers to form separate identities.

As teenagers reject their parents and their values, they create the internal space to develop their own opinions, tastes, ideals and goals. Though they may retain many aspects of their parents' views and values, they develop their own distinctive framework for them. They create who they are in the world.

Mark Twain described this transition: "When I was a boy of 14," he wrote, "my father was so ignorant I could hardly stand to have the old man around. But when I got to be 21, I was astonished at how much the old man had learned in seven years." But it could be that, in striving to step into the presidential shoes of his long-idealized older brother and his even more idealized father, Jeb somehow regressed and lost confidence in himself.

Children with powerful family members are frequently filled with self-doubt. They can feel like failures when comparing themselves to older siblings and parental figures. They might experience normal manifestations of separation or individuation—including adolescent rebellion or just the act of forming their own opinions—as if they are attacking or even killing their family members. Understandably, this causes them not just guilt but a growing fear of alienating their family.

Clinging to family love through idealization is a defensive reaction against aggressive feelings from separation and individuation. Most adolescents resolve this conflict as they realize they are merely killing off their family's controlling influence over them—not their actual family members.

If these are the psychodynamics that caused Jeb to flounder this past week, his major challenge is if and how quickly he can work through them. He has to fully recover a mind of his own—and convince the American public that he is not George W. Bush, II."

Commentary: This piece was written fifteen years after the first, and it contains many of the same psychodynamic principles: the need for idealization and the importance of de-idealization and adolescent rebellion in the service of separation–individuation. I repeated the Mark Twain quote; fifteen years had lapsed, and it was still relevant. These psychodynamic issues are enduring and will continue to repeat themselves in new presidential elections and other political contexts.

Chapter V

THE PSYCHODYNAMICS OF POLITICAL, RACIAL, RELIGIOUS AND MISOGYNISTIC HATRED

1. Hating The Politician In The Mirror *(Los Angeles Times, 1999)*

2. The "Passion" of Anti-Semitism (unpublished) (2004)

3. America's State Of Mind: Healthy And Divided
    (Los Angeles Times, 2000)

4. America's Racism: Hatred Of "The Other" In The 2008
    Presidential Election *(Huffington Post, 2008)*

5. The Hatred Between Republicans and Democrats: The Conflict
    In America's Psyche, Redux *(Huffington Post, 2008)*

6. Fiscal Cliff: D.C.'s Mayan Apocalypse
    (Thomson Reuters, 2012)

7. Does Dependency on Government Make Americans Weak?
    (Huffington Post, 2012)

8. The Puzzling Vilification of Hillary, A Psychoanalyst's
    Perspective *(Huffington Post, 2015)*

Twenty-seven years after the publication of my first op-ed piece, my second, "Hating the Politician in the Mirror," was published in the *Los Angeles Times* on January 24, 1999. I was inspired to write it by the puzzling fact that President Bill Clinton, the most Republican of all recent Democratic presidents based on his conservative political agenda, was the target of the most virulent hatred from Republicans that I had ever seen. Why wouldn't Republicans prefer him to other Democratic presidents? To explain their animosity, I used Freud's concepts of the "narcissism of minor differences," and "the superego in the service of the id." This is the piece:

Hating the Politician in the Mirror

COMMENTARY / ANALYSIS / TIMES INTERVIEW

SECTION

M

OPINION

SUNDAY
JANUARY 24, 1999

THE NATION

▶ PSYCHOLOGY

Hating the Politician in the Mirror

By Peter Wolson

Why are Republicans so hateful toward Bill Clinton when he is more like them than virtually any other Democrat? He has pushed through many of their favorite policies, such as cutting welfare, promoting the North American Free Trade Agreement and proposing that portions of Social Security reserves be privatized. You would think Republicans would regard him among their favorite Democratic presidents. Instead, the opposite is true. They seem determined to kill him politically through character assassination fueled by a hatred that is hard to understand.

Sigmund Freud had a brilliant explanation for this type of animosity: "the narcissism of minor differences." The psychoanalyst contended that human beings express their most virulent hatred toward those who are just slightly different from themselves. This is because slight differences pose a greater psychological threat to one's core sense of self (ergo "narcissism") than those who are extremely different from ourselves. Freud used this concept as an explanation for the most heinous forms of aggression.

Peter Wolson, a clinical psychologist, is director of training at the Los Angeles Institute and Society for Psychoanalytic Studies

STEVE MCAFEE for The Times

Thus, German Jews were supposed to have identified more with being German than non-Jewish Germans. The genocidal displacement of aggression toward German Jews in the Holocaust may have been partly attributable to the narcissism of minor differences, since the slight difference, the "Jewishness" of the German Jews, threatened the core identity of the German people. The same can be said of the genocide in Bosnia, the fratricidal conflict between Irish Catholics and Protestants, and the hostilities between Arabs and Israelis.

Of course, the impeachment and trial of Clinton pale by comparison with genocide and religious wars, but the same psychological principle seems to be operating. The fundamental identity of Republicans is significantly more than a flagrantly liberal Democrat.

By co-opting the Republicans' political agenda while clothed in Democratic attire, Clinton has committed the psychological crime of shattering the Republican self-structure, usurping the principles that provide them with a sense of meaning and purpose.

It is not surprising that the Republican political agenda is reportedly in shambles. From the beginning of Clinton's presidency, the Republicans' unrelenting determination to kill him politically seems to have been motivated by the need to keep the party uncontaminated by any Democratic pestilence that may resemble them, in this instance Clinton.

What better way to preserve one's distinctive identity than to show that Clinton is a sleazy, conniving, lying, cheating criminal who in no way resembles the high moral authority of the 13 Republican congressmen who are prosecuting him. In this way, the Republicans can call attention to the superiority of their party and differentiate themselves from the morally inferior threat to their political existence.

By persecuting Clinton in the name of morality, law and order, the Republicans are discharging the hatred triggered by the narcissism of minor differences. This illustrates another Freudian principle: using the superego (i.e., principles of morality, conscience, law and order) in the service of the id (i.e., sexual and aggressive impulses).

Despite a relentless "inquisition," independent counsel Kenneth W. Starr failed to expose any criminal wrongdoing on Clinton's part in Whitewater, Travelgate

and Files Tripp to revealing Like a d Clinton tr by denyin woman." The pu lied, he preassure assault in his presid avoid bel struction using the aggression and when hunters, ; for an ille; The An understoo tently hig Republica new low. Many p the Repul tinue to sl answer a; toward Cl the narcis expressed service of cans are r polls and trial with political j by the i aggressive

"Why** are Republicans so hateful toward Bill Clinton when he is more like them than virtually any other Democrat? He has pushed through many of their favorite policies, such as cutting welfare, promoting the North American Free Trade Agreement and proposing that portions of Social Security reserves be privatized. You would think Republicans would regard him among their favorite Democratic presidents. Instead, the opposite is true. They seem determined to kill him politically through character assassination fueled by a hatred that is hard to understand.

Sigmund Freud had a brilliant explanation for this type of animosity: "The narcissism of minor differences." The psychoanalyst contended that human beings express their most virulent hatred toward those who are just slightly different from themselves. This is because slight differences pose a greater psychological threat to one's core sense of self (ergo, "narcissism") than those who are extremely different from ourselves. Freud used this concept as an explanation for the most heinous forms of aggression.

Thus, German Jews were supposed to have identified more with being German than non-Jewish Germans. The genocidal displacement of aggression toward German Jews in the Holocaust may have been partly attributable to the narcissism of minor differences since the "Jewishness" of the German Jews threatened the core identity of the German people. The same can be said of the genocide in Bosnia, the fratricidal conflict between Irish Catholics and Protestants, the hostilities between Arabs and Israelis, and the genocide between the Hutus and Tutsis in Rwanda.

Of course, the impeachment and trial of Clinton pale by comparison to genocide and religious wars, but the same psychological principle seems to be operating. Clinton, as a "Republicrat," may threaten the fundamental identity of Republicans significantly more than a flagrantly liberal Democrat. By co-opting the Republicans' political agenda while clothed in Democratic attire, Clinton has committed the psychological crime of shattering the Republicans' self-structure, usurping the principles that provide them with a sense of meaning and purpose.

It is not surprising that the Republicans' political agenda is reportedly in shambles. From the beginning of Clinton's presidency, the Republicans unrelenting determination to kill him politically seems to have been motivated by the need to keep the party uncontaminated by any Democratic pestilence that may resemble them, in this instance Clinton.

What better way to preserve one's distinctive identity than to show that Clinton is a sleazy, conniving, lying, cheating criminal who in no way resembles the high moral authority of the 13 Republican congressmen who are prosecuting him. In this way, the Republicans can call attention to the superiority of their party and differentiate themselves from the morally inferior threat to their political existence.

By persecuting Clinton in the name of morality, law and order, the Republicans are discharging the hatred triggered by the narcissism of minor differences. This illustrates another Freudian principle: using the superego (i.e., principles of morality, conscience, law and order) in the service of the id (i.e., sexual and aggressive impulses).

Despite a relentless "inquisition," Independent Counsel Kenneth W. Starr failed to expose any criminal wrongdoing on Clinton's part in Whitewater, Travelgate and Filegate. He then wired Linda R. Tripp to entrap Monica S. Lewinsky into revealing her sexual liaison with Clinton. Like a deer caught in the headlights, Clinton tried to squirm out of harm's way by denying that he had sex with "that woman." He evaded being pinned down.

The public understood this. If Clinton lied, he was lying about sex under the pressure of an aggressive Republican assault in the name of morality to weaken his presidency. Calling Clinton's efforts to avoid being caught "perjury" and "obstruction of justice" is a prime example of the superego in the service of aggression. First you shoot at the deer, and when the deer tries to elude its hunters, you crucify it on moral groups for an illegitimate evasion.

The American people have intuitively understood that the Republicans are out to destroy Clinton, giving him consistently high approval ratings while the Republicans' approval ratings sank to a new low.

Many pundits are puzzled about why the Republicans would so zealously continue to shoot themselves in the feet. The answer appears to be that their hatred toward Clinton continues to be fueled by the narcissism of minor differences and expressed through the superego in the service of the id. The fact that Republicans are not heeding the warnings of the polls and are pursuing a full impeachment trial with witnesses suggests that their political judgment has become impaired by the intensity of their unconscious aggressive impulses."

Commentary: The "narcissism of minor differences" is a fascinating construct that Freud (1930) used to explain the discharge of human aggression. If one group of people is only slightly different from another, the second group poses a threat to the first group's sense of uniqueness and superiority, and vice versa. Freud cited the work of Crawley, who "declares that each individual is separated from others by a 'taboo of personal isolation,' and that it is precisely the minor differences in people who are otherwise alike that form the basis of feelings of strangeness and hostility between them."

Freud continued, "It would be tempting to pursue this idea to derive from this 'narcissism of minor differences' the hostility which in every human relation we see fighting successfully against feelings of fellowship and overpowering the commandment that all men should love one another." In other words, according to Freud, all men cannot love one another, because the narcissism of their minor differences provides an outlet for their innate aggression (Freud, 1921. page 199).

In *Civilization and Its Discontents*, Freud (1930) said, "Communities with adjoining territories and related to each other in other ways as well, who are engaged in constant feuds and in ridiculing each other, like the Spaniards and Portuguese, for instance, the North Germans and South Germans, the English and Scotch, and so on. I gave this phenomenon the name of 'the narcissism of minor differences,' a name which does not do much to explain it." He then says, "We can now see that it is a convenient and relatively harmless satisfaction to the inclination to aggression by means of which the cohesion of the community is made easier" (page 104).

Thus, at first Freud says that the narcissism of minor differences preserves a community's narcissistic self-integrity and is relatively harmless. But then he goes on to say, "In this respect, the Jewish people, scattered everywhere, have rendered more useful service to the civilization of the countries that have been their host, but unfortunately, all the massacres of Jews in the Middle Ages did not suffice to make that period more peaceful and secure for their Christian fellows. When once the Apostle Paul had posited universal love between men as the foundation of his Christian community, extreme intolerance on the part of Christiandom towards those who remained outside it, became the inevitable consequence. To the Romans who had not founded their community as a state upon love, religious intolerance was something foreign, although with them religion was a concern of the state and the state was permeated by religion, nor was it an unaccountable chance that the dream of a German world-dominion called for anti-Semitism as its complement; and it is intelligible that the attempt to establish a new communist civilization in Russia should find its psychological support in the persecution of the bourgeois. One only wonders with concern what the Soviets will do after they have wiped out their bourgeois."

We see that Freud changes from viewing the aggression discharged by the narcissism of minor differences as relatively benign to associating it with murderous anti-Semitic massacres and the purification of the identity of communist Russia by killing off the Bourgeois.

His major theory is that the "narcissism of minor differences" becomes a needed outlet for the discharge of instinctual aggression. In the Clinton piece, I elaborated his theory of the need to preserve the narcissistic cohesiveness of group identity by destroying the slightly different group, as a matter of existential survival. Clinton, as a "Republicrat" who embraced conservative principles, posed an existential threat to Republicans. In effect, they unconsciously hated him for co-opting their political identity, and arguably tried to kill him politically in order to survive. Thus, the aggression that is triggered by the narcissism of minor differences is a way to protect, strengthen and consolidate one's identity.

But Freud's notion that it is easier to project one's hatred onto someone who is slightly different from you, suggests that sameness and "familiarity breeds contempt" pose an irresistible target for ambivalence and aggression. The slightly different "other" becomes an object for projective identification, which Melanie Klein wrote about: displacing and projecting hated parts of one's self into the other, and hating them for those same qualities. It makes sense that the more similar "the other," the easier it would be to project one's own hated characteristics.

I subsequently used Freud's "narcissism of minor differences," splitting, and projective identification to explain what seemed like the main psychodynamic origins of anti-Semitism in an unpublished piece, "The 'Passion' of Anti-Semitism." This article was provoked by Mel Gibson's movie, *The Passion of the Christ*, which was released on Febtuary 24, 2004. Although not addressed in this piece, the role of envy is elaborated in the discussion that follows.

Unfortunately, anti-Semitism continues to plague the world, as evident in Charlottesville, Virginia, on August 12, 2017, in a rally of Ku Klux Klansmen and neo-Nazis bearing torches, chanting, "Jews shall not replace us!" Many feared that Mel Gibson's film, which was released on February 25th, 2004, would trigger violent anti-Semitic incidents, which were frequently the aftermath of Passion Plays, historically.

The 'Passion' of "Anti-Semitism"

"The crucial controversy over Mel Gibson's film, *The Passion of the Christ*, is not whether he made it anti-Semitic, but rather why a story about Christ's crucifixion and ressurection—a cornerstone of Christian love and forgiveness, has sparked violent hatred against Jews for centuries?

According to Christian scholars, Christ was Jewish his entire life, and Christianity started as a Jewish sect. For decades after Christ's crucifixion, his disciples continued to identify as Jewish, observed Jewish traditions, and many, including Peter and even James, Jesus's brother, wanted Christianity to remain within the Jewish community. Yet, until Pope Paul VI's second Vatican Council in 1965, *"Nostra Aetate"* ("In Our Time") proclaimed that Jews were and are not responsible for murdering Christ, the Catholic Church blamed Jews for his crucifixion dating back to the fourth century A.D. That was when Roman emperor Constantine converted from paganism to Christianity and declared that Jews were "Christ killers." Since Christ and his disciples at the time of his crucifixion were Jewish, wouldn't this virulent anti-Semitic proclamation apply to them as well?

How can we psychologically explain this nonsensical calumny?

The answer lies, in part, in what Sigmund Freud termed "the narcissism of minor differences." He pointed out that horrific aggression is often unleashed when two groups of people are virtually the same except for small variations. The similarity between the groups threatens their distinctive identities, motivating them to destroy the other in order to preserve each group's unique identity; ergo, "narcissism."

Thus, the apostle Paul of Tarsus, formerly Saul (his Jewish name), thirty-five years after Christ's crucifixion, began seeking converts to Christianity among Greek and Roman gentiles. In doing so, he blamed Jews, not Romans, for Christ's death. Historians have speculated that he did this to placate Roman authorities. But psychologically, blaming Jews had the effect of differentiating Christianity from Judaism. In other words, by making Jews the enemies of Christians in his rendition of the Passion, Paul helped to establish Christianity as a separate religion from Judaism (its parent religion).

Similarly, the Gospels of the New Testament, which were written mainly for evangelical purposes by non-witnesses decades after the crucifixion, emphasized the role of Jewish high priests, as "Christ Killers" rather than the Roman prefect, Pontius Pilate who was infamous as a brutal, crucifying despot and responsible for ordering Jesus's death. However, in the Gospel of Matthew, Pilate was portrayed as sympathetic to Christ, but acceded to the Jewish high priests' demand to kill him, to quell political dissension in the Jewish community.

The story of Christ's Passion became the centerpiece of Christianity, not just because it focused upon Jesus's preordained suffering and dying for the sins of mankind, with his resurrection paving the way for transcendental immortality, but also because it separated Christianity from Judaism by implying that traditional Mosaic Judaism was diabolical. This was suggested by Mel Gibson's hooded film image of Satan mingling with the Jewish high priests and Jewish mobs clamoring for Jesus's torture and death. Unfortunately, the subsequent "Judeo-ectomy" of Christianity has resulted in many Christians not knowing that their most revered God, his apostles, and Mary and Joseph, were all Jews at the time of Jesus's crucifixion. Many Christians are still unaware that the Last Supper was a transformed Jewish Seder, or that Christianity remained a Jewish sect for decades after Christ's death.

Another psychodynamic motivating anti-Semitism among Christians relates to the difficulty of embracing Christ's message of replacing hatred with universal love. As Freud stated, it is difficult to accept both hatred and love at the same time, and much easier to split the two by seeing "others" as either "all good" or "all bad." For Christians, this would mean being morally compelled to love the Jews and Romans they hated for murdering Christ. They are morally obliged to accept themselves as sinners, like the "Christ-killing" Jews. After all, Christ told them he died for their sins.

So what happens to their hatred when Christians must deny and replace it with love? Freud suggested that it becomes disowned, displaced and projected into the Jewish "other." Christians hate Jews for murdering Christ as a scapegoat for the sins they hate in themselves.

Such projective identification might have influenced Paul of Tarsus in his conversion to Christianity and subsequent animosity toward Jews. Before his conversion, Paul was a violent Christian-hating Jewish Pharisee who persecuted, imprisoned and executed Christians. After converting to Christianity, he appears to have disowned and projected his hatred of Christians into Jews and then condemned them for being Christ killers, rather than owning and holding himself responsible for his former Christian-killing self. Thus, the hatred of Jews, motivated by "the narcissism of minor differences" and projective identification, made Christianity more cohesive as a separate religion from Judaism and provided an outlet for the pent-up aggression caused by Christ's commandment to replace hatred with universal love.

This could explain why Passion Plays have historically evoked violence instead of love toward Jews. Based on his personal behavior and the screenplay of *The Passion*, Mel Gibson appears to be struggling with integrating the split between love and hate in his own psyche. On the one hand, he professes Christian love for everyone, including Jews, and on the other, rejects Vatican II's retraction of Jewish blame for Christ's crucifixion and refuses to differentiate himself from his father's anti-Semitism. Gibson's *The Passion*, like the Passion Plays of old, reflects this paradox? Though he consciously intends to disseminate Christ's message of love and forgiveness, he is also providing an outlet for the traditional Christian hatred toward Jews as Christ killers."

Commentary: Anti-Semitism might also be an expression of repressed hatred toward Christ, who was himself a vilified and persecuted Jew. Freud speculated that Christians might envy Jews for having the freedom to reject and hate Christ, which the commandment of universal love considers sinful. My friend and colleague, Dr. Alan Spivak, wondered if religions that tolerate more freedom of thought, including anger toward their own religion, might be more tolerant of other religions and less scapegoating. This would provide the outlet for aggression that Freud thought was needed for Christ's message of loving the enemies you hate. You also need to tolerate hating the ones you love.

It should be noted that Martin Luther, the leader of the Protestant Reformation, never considered Jews to be Christ killers, but hated them for rejecting his efforts to convert them to Christianity. When he learned that some Jews were trying to convert Christians to Judaism, he exhorted his followers to persecute them harshly. This hatred might have been fueled by the narcissism of minor differences, since he didn't expect such conversions from Muslims and Buddhists (religions that were markedly different from Christianity). This anti-Semitic tradition in German Lutheranism might have facilitated the German people's acceptance of genocide against the Jews under Hitler.

Fortunately, Gibson's *The Passion of the Christ* did not induce outbreaks of anti-Semitic violence, but in the last few years, such incidents have increased, especially in Europe. In the first three months of 2017, anti-Semitic activity in the US rose 86% compared with a comparable period in 2016. In 2017, a synagogue in Gothenberg, Sweden, was firebombed, and a mob in Malmo, Sweden, chanted, "We are going to shoot Jews," *(Financial Times,* December 10, 2017). Anti-Semitic incidents in Berlin rose 16% in 2016 over 2015 *(Financial Times,* December 15, 2017), and in France there were threats to burn down a synagogue in Paris, a slashing of a Jewish girl's face, and displays of swastika graffiti after President Trump recognized Jerusalem as the capital of Israel *(The Times of Israel,* January 20, 2018).

The Charlottesville neo-Nazi chant, "Jews shall not replace us," suggests the role of envy as another insidious cause of anti-Semitism. Widespread envy over the ages has probably been triggered by the Old Testament depiction of the Jews as God's "chosen people," which excludes others from God's special love.

According to Kleinian theory, envy is the most virulent source of human aggression. In the case of anti-Semitism, envy of European Jews in the Middle Ages for their success in lending and banking exacerbated Christian anti-Semitism, which left them on the periphery of society, forced into ghettos, excluded from citizenship and frequently expelled from host countries. Jewish massacres were commonplace, fueled by hateful fantasies of greedy usurers, inhuman spawns of the devil, evil perpetrators of the black plague, and drinking the blood of Christian children.

In the 20th and 21st centuries, Jews were envied for their disproportionate success in business, finance, the arts, sciences, entertainment and virtually every other field of intellectual endeavor. Three Jews—Albert Einstein, Sigmund Freud and Karl Marx—were widely acclaimed as the most influential people in the world. Yet the Jewish population in most countries, probably due to anti-Semitism and the Jewish antipathy toward proselytizing, has been exceedingly small, comprising only 2.2% of the American population. Recently, envy-based conspiracy fantasies of Jews insidiously controlling finance and literally running the world, have proliferated with Jewish Billionaire George Soros portrayed as the greedy, omnipotent devil financing a caravan of rapists, criminals and terrorists to invade America (October, 2018). The Nazi Holocaust and the numerous massacres, pogroms and continual eruptions of anti-Semitic violence throughout the ages suggest that Jews were and remain the most hated religious group in the world. In 2016, more than 50% of all American religious hate crimes were against

Jews versus 16% against Muslims *(Huffington Post,* Uri Wilensky, February 26, 2016). Muslim hatred of Jews has been largely triggered by the establishment of the State of Israel in the Arab Middle East. Many Arab Muslims view Israel as a symbol of the Christian Crusaders fighting against Islam during the Middle Ages in what both terrorists and, unfortunately, President Donald Trump, have characterized as a war between civilizations.

Ironically, most Christians today support Israel as the foundation of Christianity and respect Jews as God's "chosen people." However, the psychodynamics of the narcissism of minor differences, splitting, projective identification and envy in distinguishing Christianity from Judaism has historically unleashed a virulent anti-Semitic pestilence that continues to infect countries throughout the world, including Myanmar and Japan, which have virtually no exposure to Jews.

The hatred between Republicans and Democrats is the subject of my next piece. Toward the end of the presidential election campaign between Al Gore and George W. Bush, there was a virtual fifty–fifty split between Republicans and Democrats in Congress. This gridlock could continue unabated and could obstruct congressional progress, or it could compel congressmen to compromise for the good of America. To predict the outcome, I speculated about what internal objects Republicans and Democrats represented within the American psyche.

The following op-ed piece was published in the *Los Angeles Times* on November 26, 2000.

America's State of Mind: Healthy and Divided

SECTION

M

SUNDAY
NOVEMBER 26, 2000 / NA

OPINION

Los Angeles Times

THE NATION

America's State of Mind: Healthy and Divided

▶ SOCIETY

By Peter Wolson

In this time of prosperity and with both political parties moving toward the center, how can we account for the fifty-fifty partisan standoff in America's body politic? Both houses of Congress are almost evenly divided between Republicans and Democrats, and the presidential race has come down to fewer than 1,000 votes in Florida. One might think that as the two parties moved closer to the center, the chances for political deadlock would have dropped. But the opposite has occurred. Why?

Broadly speaking, in the American psyche, the Democratic Party's vision of government is roughly equivalent to a powerful, nurturing mother figure protecting and caring for the needy and downtrodden. By contrast, the Republican ideal embodies a strong father figure who rewards people for taking responsibility for their own lives and who supports independent initiative. The Democratic "breast-mother" government satisfies the basic human need to be taken care of by a loving, tolerant parent; the Republican father figure fulfills the need to break from parental domination, to have control over one's life and to pursue one's fortune.

Psychologically, the basic human need of maternal nurturance often conflicts

Peter Wolson is a psychoanalyst and past

with the need for autonomy. During adolescence, this conflict plays out: Children struggle to liberate themselves from their need for parental care by rebelling against parental authority and trying to assume personal responsibility for their lives. However, even after the adolescent has attained adulthood and become more self-reliant, the psychological need to be taken care of persists to varying degrees and remains in conflict with the need for separation and autonomy. In the political arena, Americans try to resolve this personal

MARTIN GUNSAULLUS/For The Times

Americans who have traditionally been more in need of help or care—women, the working class, the aged, the disabled, immigrants, certain racial and religious minorities, gays, etc.—and Americans who support them are more likely to vote Democratic. For these voters, liberal means the generosity of a nurturing governing structure. In contrast, they view Republicans as uncaring, hardhearted and greedy, a party of the rich and powerful demanding that government support their aggressive, self-serving (often entrepre-

"In this time of prosperity and with both political parties moving toward the center, how can we account for the fifty–fifty partisan stand-off in America's body politic? Both houses of Congress are almost evenly divided between Republicans and Democrats, and the presidential race has come down to fewer than 1000 votes in Florida. One might think that as the two parties moved closer to the center, the chances for political deadlock would have dropped. But the opposite has occurred. Why?

Broadly speaking, in the American psyche, the Democratic Party's vision of government is roughly equivalent to a powerful, nurturing mother figure protecting and caring for the needy and downtrodden. By contrast, the Republican ideal embodies a strong father figure who rewards people for taking responsibility for their own lives and who supports independent initiative. The Democratic "breast-mother" government satisfies the basic human need to be taken care of by a loving tolerant parent; the Republican father figure fulfills the need to break away from parental domination, to have control over one's life and pursue one's fortune.

Psychologically, the basic human need for maternal nurturance often conflicts with the need for autonomy. During adolescence, this conflict plays out. Children struggle to liberate themselves from their need for parental care by rebelling against parental authority and trying to assume personal responsibility for their lives. However, even after the adolescent has attained adulthood and become more self-reliant, the psychological need to be taken care of persists to varying degrees and remains in conflict with the need for separation and autonomy. In the political arena, Americans try to resolve this personal conflict by voting for the party that represents their strongest internal need.

Americans who have traditionally been more in need of help or care— women, the working class, the aged, the disabled, immigrants, certain racial and religious minorities, gays, etc.—and Americans who support them, are more likely to vote Democratic. For these voters, *liberal* means the generosity of a nurturing governing structure. In contrast, they view Republicans as uncaring, hardhearted and greedy, a party of the rich and powerful, demanding that government support their aggressive, self-serving (often entrepreneurial) needs.

For liberal Democrats, *conservative* is often equated with depriving the hungry and poor of government support through tax dodges, paying employees the lowest wages and benefits they can get away with, exploiting "mother earth" for profit, and risking gun violence for the macho preference to hunt. They view the Republican stance against abortion as a willingness to ruin a woman's life in favor of the right of a fetus to live, again supporting the vital interests of a "child" against a "murderous" maternal authority.

In contrast, Americans who live according to an ethic of self-reliance and subscribe to the right of an individual to control his own life, money and property with minimal interference, are more likely to vote for a paternal Republican government. For these voters, government represents a powerful, controlling paternal figure, a necessary evil that potentially threatens individual autonomy by "stealing" earned money through excessive taxes. The ideal Republican governance does not spoil or infantilize the people with nurturing protective handouts but requires them to be responsible for themselves and supports individual initiative through tax breaks.

If Democrats and Republicans signify, respectively, the human need to be taken care of versus the need for autonomy and control, then the fifty-fifty split in the 2000 campaign suggests that both basic psychological needs are exceptionally well represented in the American body politic. In other words, the American psyche is maximally healthy. Yet, as a result of this desirable balance, the political process seems deadlocked.

Will this continue, and is this bad or good for America? The current psychological stability of the country, perhaps more than at any other time, gives each party's politicians the choice of moving forward or remaining paralyzed. A fifty–fifty split means that the only way for each party to fulfill its political agenda is to compromise with the needs of the other. Ideally, this would lead to more balanced political programs and great satisfaction for the American people.

But government might also remain stalemated by partisan politics. In other words, elected politicians might self-destructively choose not to compromise. This would frustrate the American people, having made the best psychological selection for themselves, but electing politicians unwilling to make concessions necessary to fulfill their needs.

Unfortunately, America cannot avoid this conflict. U.S. politics will inevitably be divisive because of the inherent unconscious conflict between the need to be taken care of, as represented by Democrats, and the desire for autonomy and control, embodied by Republicans. It is the dynamic struggle between these two competing psychological needs that serves as a major catalyst for human growth, both individually and politically. Ironically, the most representative election outcome provides the greatest opportunity to fulfill the psychological wishes of the American people, while also leaving them ripe for political deadlock."

Commentary: Wow! Is this 2018? Eighteen years later, and we are still plagued by this issue. Unfortunately, political deadlock has continued and worsened over the years, largely due to the narcissism of minor (and major) differences between tribal groups within each political party. The underlying, festering problem of America appears to be its increasing, inexorable diversity of political beliefs, ethnicity, race, religion and gender. In addition to the internal conflict between dependency and autonomy, a large portion of the hatred between Republicans and Democrats is attributable to hatred of "the other," a dynamic that is deeply embedded in the human psyche.

This dynamic was the centerpiece of a blog published in the *Huffington Post* on October 16, 2008, three weeks before black Senator Barack Obama defeated a white, American war hero, Senator John McCain, for the presidency by an overwhelming margin.

America's Racism: Hatred of "The Other" in the 2008 Presidential Election

"Considering the dire state of the economy, health care, Iraq and global warming after eight years of the Bush administration, the Democratic presidential candidate, Barack Obama, should have had a substantial lead over his Republican adversary, John McCain, from the beginning of the campaign, but didn't. The race has been neck and neck, with Obama leading in recent polls largely because of the economic crisis.

Increasingly, pundits and politicians, like David Gergen (after the second debate) and former San Francisco Mayor Willie Brown, are attributing the closeness of this election to racial prejudice, what some call "The Bradley Effect." This alludes to 1982 exit polls favoring black candidate for California's governor, Tom Bradley, which turned out to be shockingly wrong when his white opponent, George Deukmejian, beat him in the election. The same phenomenon occurred in the political races of black candidates David Dinkins in New York City and Douglas Wilder in Virginia. Recent polls in key states like Ohio, Michigan, West Virginia, Kentucky and Indiana reveal that racism accounts for at least twenty per cent of the vote against Obama. The true figure is probably 30%. Fox News (9/22/08) reported that only 70% of Democrats support Barack Obama, while 85% of Republicans support John McCain. Moreover, 33% of Democrats have negative attitudes toward blacks, which translates into 6% of the national vote. Thus, racism could decide the outcome of the election.

In view of white America's traditional racism since slavery, Obama's candidacy shows enormous racial progress. Obama himself considers racism a "wash" when comparing those voting for him because he is black and those who hold it against him. But pervasive fears of his assassination, incorrectly stereotyping him as a Muslim, considering him an uppity elitist, or the question, "Is our country ready for a black president?" suggest that racism can cause him to lose the election.

Psychologically, racism stems from the primordial hatred of "the other" that is deeply embedded in our mind from birth. We begin life in the womb, physically and psychologically merged with our mother, sharing common nutrition and oxygen through her blood supply. If we could place ourselves in the fetus's psyche, this merged state is probably experienced as paradise since we are completely taken care of without having to do anything for ourselves. There is no difference between our internal mental world and the external physical world. When the umbilical cord is cut, we are physically separated from mother, but we are still psychologically merged with her. We experience everything, including the external world, as our self. Psychoanalyst Sigmund Freud called this primary narcissism.

However, at birth, our enwombed paradise is shattered as we are bombarded by light, noise, hunger and pain—for the first time. We experience aversive stimulation, the first representation of "the other," as frustrating threats to our existence, and become enraged. To watch a frustrated baby is like observing an angry demi-god with little lighting bolts coming out of its head.

Our hatred of "the other" continues unconsciously throughout development. At the youngest ages, we idealize our parents as the best parents in the world and react to strangers with trepidation and anger. We experience our religion as superior to all others and tend to hate strange religions, we believe that our race is superior and hate other races, or believe that our nation is the greatest and hate other nations. Hating "the other" is a way of protecting our original, archaic merged state within mother's womb that still unconsciously exists in our mental life. If you add to this the strangeness of someone of a different race, such as black Americans who start out as slaves, our fear and hatred increase exponentially. American families grow up with traditions of hatred against "others." "You've got to be carefully taught to hate and fear," the South Pacific song goes, whether it is whites hating blacks or vice versa.

The "other" is like an unknown stimulus, like a Rorschach onto which it is easy to disown and project dehumanizing evil and depraved behaviors. For example, hating our own sexual, licentious impulses, unconsciously projecting them onto blacks, and accusing them of being sexually depraved. Thus McCain's accusation against Obama of crossing boundaries in promoting sex education for kindergarten children while showing Obama smiling lasciviously in ads, appeals to unconscious racism based on projective identification. Or the Republican portrayal of Obama as a terrorist when McCain and Palin, in desperation from their plunge in the polls, may want to terrorize him.

Or we could project what we hate about our internal parents, such as a hated, dominating father—a typical Democratic depiction of McCain as a cranky authoritarian curmudgeo—or the Republican portrayal of a Democratic-run government as a suffocating, indulgent mother.

The antidote for our hatred of "the other" is empathy. As the country learns more about Barack Obama, for example, his upbringing and family, and sees how black families are the same as white families, with good values, struggling with the same human issues and reflecting so much of what is good about humanity, the prospect of having a black family in what has exclusively been the "White" House becomes increasingly conceivable and acceptable. Through empathic familiarity, the fear and hatred of the "other" and the toxic projections of "badness" often dissolve into seeing and loving the other like ourselves and as part of the human family. By identifying with the "other," we resonate with that archaic state of enwombment and pleasurable merger that is embedded so deeply within our psyches that "the other" becomes us. We are "the other."

Commentary: The fear of "the other" didn't stop Obama from defeating McCain handily. However, the gridlock between Republicans and Democrats worsened, with Senate majority leader Mitch O'Connell vowing to defeat President Obama's agenda at any cost.

It should be noted that the fear and hatred of "the other" is motivated by the "narcissism of major differences." As my colleague, Dr. Alan Spivak, pointed out, the mother's "otherness," even when just slightly mal-attuned, is probably experienced by the baby as a major existential threat to its omnipotence and primary narcissism.

On November 20, 2008 in the *Huffington Post*, I revisited the issue of the hatred between Republicans and Democrats, elaborating on the developmental psychodynamics concerning the hatred of "others."

The Hatred Between Republicans and Democrats: The Conflict Within America's Psyche, Redux

"In a previous blog posted on October 16th, 2008, I described how racism in the 2008 presidential campaign is largely the result of a hatred and fear of "the other" that is deeply embedded within the human psyche from birth. "The other" is often an ambiguous stimulus upon which we can project disowned and hated parts of ourselves and hated internal parental figures. These psychodynamics also apply to the hatred between Republicans and Democrats, evidenced by the venomous stereotyping of Republicans by Democrats and of Democrats by Republicans. For example, Pat Buchanan, on *The Chris Matthews Show*, largely attributed Colin Powell's support of Barack Obama to racism.

Even mental health professionals, most of whom are liberal, often cannot believe how Republicans can possibly think and feel as they do, hatefully stereotyping them as virtual Nazis, and have used conferences to scapegoat Republicans in the name of deepening psychological understanding of political processes. This is amazing since psychotherapists are professional empathizers, who put themselves in the shoes of others every day. Yet so many of them have difficulty placing themselves in the shoes of nearly 50% of the American population. And I am as guilty as anyone. The Simon Wiesenthal Center for the study of intolerance points out that we are all prejudiced, and must accept this fact, in order to confront it within ourselves to modulate its toxic influence."

In the rest of the piece, I quoted the article I presented above, "America's State of Mind: Healthy and Divided," focusing on the public's intrapsychic conflict between the autonomous paternal psychic representation of the Republican Party and the caretaking maternal representation of the Democratic Party, as contributing to the political hatred between parties. I end the current *Huffington Post* piece with:

"Let us hope that the catastrophic domestic and world situation confronting the new President and Congress is sufficiently motivating to repair America's devastated psyche by overcoming the vitriolic hatred of 'the other' and by ameliorating the self-destructive conflict between dependency and autonomy."

The self-destructive rigid adherence to political ideology, whether for Democrats or Republicans, is illustrated in the next piece, "Fiscal Cliff: The D.C. Mayan Apocalypse," published in *Thomson Reuters* on December 20, 2012. In this article, I explored the psychodynamics of apocalyptic psychology and Leon Festinger's theory of cognitive dissonance, to explain why Congress would support economic policies that could potentially bring America to the brink of economic collapse on December 21, 2012, the same day as the prognosticated Mayan apocalypse. Some interpreted this as the day when the world was supposed to end. I compared the hateful destructiveness of congressional gridlock to this veritable "end of days" scenario, and speculated about its possible unconscious functions.

Fiscal Cliff: D.C.'s Mayan Apocalypse

"We are careening toward Dec. 21, 2012, the date of the Mayan apocalypse, when the world is supposed to come to an end through a series of cataclysmic upheavals, according to assorted astrologers and mystics—though not the Mayans themselves, who said it was merely the end of their calendar. We are also hurtling toward the Jan. 1 "fiscal cliff," when the American economy could re-enter a devastating recession—a man-made mini-apocalypse.

What has motivated people, across so many civilizations and centuries, to devise and believe in an apocalypse? Understanding this might help us address the ideological gridlock now propelling Republicans and Democrats toward this fiscal "end of days."

There have always been groups who believe in a coming apocalypse, suggesting this is inherent in human nature. People who experience life as traumatic, devastating or chaotic are prone to project such nihilistic visions onto the world at large. Anxiety about one's own death can also evoke a catastrophic apprehension about the end of the entire world.

Yet virtually every story of the apocalypse contains a belief in a rebirth or renewal just before or after the end of days. The apocalypse destroys all that is bad in life, wiping the slate clean for a second chance—like the Second Coming of the Messiah.

This is particularly true in the Judeo-Christian tradition. In the Book of Revelations, the apocalypse is a battle between good and evil, in which the earthly world is destroyed and replaced by an otherworldly paradise. In the New Testament, the horrific pain of existence is replaced by the second chance of being resurrected and joining Jesus, God the Father and the angels in an eternal heaven. In this way, one's life and death represent a personal apocalypse—a precursor to an afterlife in heaven.

This wish for renewal could be the unconscious motivation of the astrologers who predicted the Mayan apocalypse—and the unconscious motivation of the Washington Republicans and Democrats, who seem ready to throw the American economy off the fiscal cliff in the service of their ideological beliefs.

In his classic 1956 study on "cognitive dissonance," University of California Professor Leon Festinger found that when these apocalyptic predictions are not borne out, the believers actually become more convinced that their doomsday scenario is valid. For example, when the apocalypse did not occur on the day predicted, Festinger found that the members of the apocalyptic cult rationalized that because they were true believers, God had spared them—and postponed the end of the world.

This reduced the discomfiting dissonance between their expectation and reality. That the predictions failed to come true only served to strengthen the cult's convictions and re-energize their recruiting efforts.

So maybe we should look at the fiscal cliff as, in effect, a man-made mini-apocalypse. It's both answered prayer and worst nightmare for Democrats and Republicans—especially when the United States is so economically fragile. If the American economy plunges over the cliff, to the horror of both parties, there would be higher taxes not just on the richest 2 percent but for the entire middle class. There would also be radical spending cuts that could cause greater unemployment and push us back into recession. Though polls reflect that Republicans will be blamed, President Barack Obama and the Democrats could also be held responsible.

For each party, to compromise is "cognitively dissonant," negating and disconfirming its political values, a severe blow to its ideological pride, honor and self-esteem. But to rigidly cling to one's political ideology to avoid cognitive dissonance at the expense of the country's economic welfare, even at the expense of one's political survival, places politicians' ideological self-interests above the common good.

In response to the pressure of the apocalyptic fiscal cliff, the Republicans and Democrats will either remain deadlocked and go over. Or, like Festinger's apocalyptic cult, they will rationalize a way to compromise while preserving and strengthening their political beliefs.

In this way, while bringing us to the brink of devastation, they might foster an economic renaissance. In psychological terms, the creation of the fiscal cliff might well have been motivated by an unconscious wish for renewal. Or, at least, as astrologers and mystics believe in their myth of the Mayan apocalypse, we would like to believe this is so."

Commentary: It is now 2018, and congressional gridlock continues unabated. Republicans control the presidency and both houses of Congress, yet they can hardly pass any bills because of their ideological battles with Democrats and within their own party. Tribal ideologies of moderates and extremists in both parties have obstructed compromise on health care, climate change, taxes, immigration, infrastructure, etc.

The notion of destroying everything that has gone wrong with one's past as a prelude to a rebirth is a time-worn unconscious defensive strategy. Depressive nihilism in patients, for example, often serves a similar purpose. Nothing can be worse than the way they have felt, yet their nihilism defends against the vulnerability of hope, the possibility of overwhelming unbearable disappointment in trying to make their lives better. Because they have already experienced too much pain to tolerate any more, nihilism comes to the rescue. By retreating from life and hating the world and everything in it, they unconsciously protect themselves from being hurt again, since nothing can be worse than the depressive pain they have felt before.

Paradoxically, depressive nihilism is often motivated by unconscious idealism. Anything short of one's ideal world doesn't feel worth the emotional price. Nihilistic despair is often a reaction to how little the world fulfills one's fantasy of how life should ideally be. By giving up on life, the nihilist preserves this fantasy, as if unconsciously declaring, "I refuse to be hopeful and refuse to make my life better unless the world is the way I want it."

Short of a miraculous spurt of psychological maturity in resolving tribal splitting and identity politics, a devastating political apocalypse might motivate our gridlocked Congressional parties to make productive concessions that lead to pragmatic legislation that benefits America as a whole instead of narcissistic fiefdoms. America is still waiting for salvation. Let's hope it's not waiting for Godot!

In the 2012 presidential contest between Republican Governor George Romney and Democratic President Barack Obama, one of Romney's main conservative attacks against Democratic liberals was that dependency on government made Americans weak. When Romney said that 47% of Americans were afflicted with this weakness, he arguably wrote his presidential epitaph. He didn't understand that healthy dependency is as psychologically necessary as healthy autonomy and self-reliance. I addressed this issue in a blog for the *Huffington Post* published on October 1, 2012.

Does Dependency on Government Make Americans Weak? A Psychoanalyst's Perspective

"In the last weeks of the campaign, the battle between Mitt Romney and Barack Obama has increasingly focused on the psychological consequences of dependency on government. Mitt Romney claims that the 47% of Americans who rely on government services, like Social Security and Medicare, refuse to be responsible for their own lives and feel like victims. Reflecting Republican ideology, he believes that government support fosters pathological dependency, by which he means infantile longings to be taken care of, instead of the motivation to fend for oneself. He argues that by reducing government entitlements, Americans would have to become more self-reliant, which would strengthen their character.

Is this true? Does dependency on others lead to regression and weaken one's character?

From a psychoanalytic perspective, developmental experiences of healthy dependency are essential for a person to become a self-reliant, independent adult. In fact, most psychoanalysts would argue that there is no such thing as pure independence. People who depend exclusively upon themselves and are unable to depend on others suffer from a form of pathological narcissism. These individuals feel that any dependency on others weakens them and makes them vulnerable to the power and control of the caregiver. Often they have been victims of traumatic parental deprivation as children. Consequently, they cannot take in love, nurturance or protection without feeling extremely threatened. Most psychoanalysts are engaged in helping these individuals begin to trust and depend on others once again.

In business, an example of pathological narcissism would be an entrepreneur who refuses to take a loan from parents or a bank, or use credit in any way, even to start a new business or salvage one that is failing, for fear that such dependency on others for financial support would weaken him. Clearly, most businessmen and government leaders do not fall into this category. They believe that dependency on others for credit and loans is necessary for the success of their businesses. Similarly, Paul Ryan, who argues against dependency on government, asked for and thankfully received financial help from the federal government to assist workers who were displaced from the closing of a GM plant in his congressional district of Janesville, Wisconsin.

Obviously, poor children who need school lunches, families who need food stamps and have no means of earning money, the disabled who cannot afford medical care, like Ryan's faltering automobile industry, need government help to survive and to have a minimal floor of financial and medical stability for them to better their lives.

Are retirees who have paid taxes for Social Security and Medicare throughout their careers entitled to the money and the services they have invested in? These are not government handouts to irresponsible people. Social Security would be financially viable if not for the fact that members of Congress have raided the Social Security treasury to pay for personal vested interests, like earmarks in their states and other government projects, thereby depleting these reserves and placing the entire Social Security program in jeopardy.

However, there is no doubt that some people are pathologically dependent on government handouts. While in graduate school, I recall a small rural town in which virtually every inhabitant was on some form of Social Security Disability, food stamps or other types of welfare. Town residents would tell you that you were a fool if you worked for a living when you could get the government to take care of you. Pathological dependency often derives from over-indulgence in childhood, in which you were spoiled by your parents and never had to fend for yourself, or from extreme deprivation in which you were grossly neglected and lacked basic parental caretaking. As adults, the overindulged would feel entitled to be taken care of because that is what they were used to, and the neglected and deprived would feel entitled to compensation for the unjust deprivation they had to endure.

Fortunately, Americans who are pathologically dependent on government support are relatively few compared to most Americans who genuinely need government services. Bill Clinton introduced a program to wean people off welfare by inducing them to find work. Democrats on the radical left objected to this as too harshly conservative. Clinton's program could be characterized as a form of parental guidance, helping the welfare recipient become self-reliant, as would a good parent. But this was another form of government dependency; that is, dependency on a program that fostered financial independence.

The ultimate challenge for Americans is to find a balance between healthy dependence on government and personal independence. The extreme polarization of the Democrats and the Republicans on this issue is a symptom of the failure to recognize that healthy dependency and healthy independence are inextricably intertwined and that both are vital for healthy psychological functioning."

Commentary: The notion that dependency is weak is built into an American ethos of rugged individualism. This is arguably derived from a culture of masculine domination and misogyny. It exhorts Americans to be independent and self-reliant, like strong men, whereas it depicts dependency as feminine and weak. The irony is that what appears to be strength in men is frequently defensive compensation for fears of weakness. Thus, many men are burdened with having to appear strong and invulnerable because they lack sufficient masculine self-confidence to reveal their vulnerability and deeper feelings. In striking contrast, many confident athletes feel free to embrace and even kiss their teammates after a victory and weep after losing or even winning a critical contest in front of a nationwide audience.

A president with fears of inadequacy can try to compensate by hiding behind a hyper-testosterone "macho" persona that can potentially endanger our country. This seemed to be happening at the start of George W. Bush's presidential administration. He was initially depicted as stupid, weak and inept by the media, but after the 9/11 terrorist attack against the World Trade Center in New York, he attempted to project a powerful masculine image, declaring war on terrorism and acting like a sheriff determined to catch the "evil-doers"—"dead or alive." He even called himself "the decider" (in contrast to appearing dumbfounded when the attack first occurred) and, without waiting for UN verification of Iraqi nuclear preparations, initiated a war against Iraq.

Similarly, this appears to be a major danger of President Trump's thin skin—hypersensitivity to criticism and fear of being perceived as a loser. This might cause him to impulsively start a nuclear war with North Korea's Kim Jong Un in order to appear strong. The most important point of my article on dependency is that healthy independence and self-reliance are based on having had sufficient experiences of healthy dependency and internalizing parental caretaking. This internalization of a supportive inner parent contributes to a strong, confident sense of self and the capacity to shift adaptively between independence and dependence as needed throughout one's lifetime. It is obviously necessary that our political leaders have a capacity for healthy dependency and self-reliance and are not compelled to compensate for feelings of inadequacy and intimidation by acting like a bully by increasing our nuclear stockpile or impulsively starting a war.

Unlike racial, religious and political hatred, hatred of women has different psychodynamics. The extreme hatred and distrust of Hillary Clinton by men and women of both parties in the 2016 presidential election provided an excellent opportunity to explore the psychodynamic basis for endemic misogyny in the human psyche. The next piece was timely and became my most widely read article. It was published in the *Huffington Post* on May 27, 2016, and garnered 107,000 "likes" on Facebook.

The Puzzling Vilification of Hillary,
A Psychoanalyst's Perspective

"How can we explain the virulent hatred toward Hillary Clinton from men and women of both political parties? The attacks against her: Benghazi, personal emails, lying, etc., are relatively minor, the usual political scuttlebutt, in contrast to the extreme intensity of her vilification. So many people say they just don't like her, and this negative impression is not new. Since her role as First Lady in Bill Clinton's White House, she has been portrayed as a witch, a Lady Macbeth, a ruthlessly ambitious, egocentric woman who considers herself above the law to achieve her exploitative goals. Some see her as a shrieking harpy. As a psychoanalyst, I believe that the intensity of this character assassination is motivated by a largely unconscious misogyny that is deeply rooted in the human (male and female) psyche. It is often triggered in response to a strong, independent woman. But this enmity is especially intense for Hillary, who is emotionally reserved and aggressive in her pursuit of the presidency. (See SNL's recent hilarious caricatures of these qualities.)

None of her caring activities have dispelled the impression that she is cold and inhuman. Not her steadfast work on behalf of children. Not her unwavering support of women: their reproductive rights and equal pay, and her advocacy for disadvantaged minorities: blacks and Hispanics. Not her exemplary role as a wife, who remained faithful to her philandering husband, nor her role as a loving mother to her daughter, Chelsea.

Male presidential contenders like Bernie Sanders and Donald Trump can act strongly, ambitiously, strategically and aggressively, and the public admires them for these traits rather than demanding "emotional warmth." As a cool-tempered woman, Hillary is judged by a different standard. In 2008, it was only when she broke down crying at a coffee house campaign stop that she was perceived as capable of feeling.

What upsets so many Americans about a strong, competitive woman? In the corporate world, such women are often seen as castrators, trying to act like men and steal masculine power for themselves. The classic psychoanalytic explanation has been "penis envy." Theoretically, this motivates a woman to disavow her feminine passive receptivity and become cold and castrating, to compensate for her lack of phallic power.

While some women might struggle with this conflict, the theory of penis envy has been largely discredited in contemporary psychoanalytic circles as a reflection of Freud's male chauvinism and misinterpretation of female anatomy. In my opinion, a more convincing explanation involves the enormous importance of mothers to their babies. At the most vulnerable time of their lives, babies are completely dependent on their mothers for psychic and physical survival. No one will ever have more power over them. Fathers, at best, are background, supportive figures. A cold, unresponsive, rejecting mother can threaten a baby's existence and elicit extreme self-protective rage. I believe that Hillary's coolness and ambitious assertiveness has evoked this unconscious primordial dread, resulting in her highly unfavorable ratings.

But this is not the entire explanation. As young children, we depend so heavily upon maternal caretaking that both boys and girls must wean and separate themselves to become independent and self-reliant. According to psychoanalyst Ralph Greenson, we often do this by dis-identifying with her, disparaging our need for mother as weak, and by devaluing mothers as emotional, unreasonable and inferior to men. This deep-seated misogyny is manifested in the cultural discrimination against women worldwide, and the traditional belief that they should serve exclusively as nurturing, maternal caretakers and be dominated by their fathers and husbands. Arguably, the most extreme misogyny is evident in Muslim countries in which women must hide their faces and bodies in burkas and serve men as sexual possessions with no independent voice.

The objectification of women as sexual objects is part of this deni-gration. Thus, Donald Trump insists that women must be rated as 10s to have any value. Even Ed Rendell, a former Democratic governor of Pennsylvania and staunch supporter of Hillary Clinton, predicted in a recent interview with the *Washington Post*, that Donald Trump's judg-ment of women's looks will backfire against him. Rendell reasoned, "There are probably more ugly women in America than attractive women. People take that stuff personally." He was oblivious to his own misogyny in this statement. In the media, Hillary is often viciously mocked for her hairdos, wearing only pant suits and looking matronly, while Bernie Sanders, with his bald pate surrounded by unkempt white hair is rarely criticized for his appearance.

The outrageous irony, in my opinion, is that such universal misogyny is the way that men, and to a lesser extent women, unconsciously protect themselves from the primordial fear of the awesome, vital power of their mothers in infancy. A reserved, ambitious woman like Hillary evokes this unconscious dreaded visage that threatens our psychic existence and engenders defensive hatred.

In a *New York Times* op-ed piece (May 22, 2016), Elizabeth Word Gutting said about Hillary: "...she is always the last woman standing. She has survived ceaseless attacks. It must get very tiring and yet she never flags....Sometimes I think that many people in this country are still scared to see a powerful woman." Unfortunately, the struggle against unconscious discrimination against strong women persists, even with the possible election of the first female president. We must all have the patience and fortitude, much like Hillary, to continue fighting against this insidious bias and ultimately extinguish it."

Commentary: Hillary Clinton was shocked, as were so many other Americans, liberals as well as conservatives, by her unpredictable loss to Donald Trump. Previews of her new book, *What Happened*, say that she blames misogyny, James Comey and Bernie Sanders, but ultimately her-self for mistakes she made. In the book, she reportedly criticizes herself for making paid speeches to Wall Street banks as "bad optics"; she calls her use of a private email server "Dumb."

Many Americans disliked her for blaming others, making excuses or justifications and taking weeks before assuming some responsibility for questionable activities. For example, she castigated the women Bill had sex with rather than him, her response to Benghazi was laggard and insensitive, and she called Trump's blue-collar supporters "deplorables." But she blamed herself for not anticipating Trump's reality-TV-style campaigning, which fueled widespread rage toward the political establishment, and blamed her own team for not devising an effective way to combat it. Nor did she give sufficient importance to the millions of blue-collar workers who were leaving the Democratic Party, feeling unheard and neglected.

I relished this piece as an opportunity to create a psychoanalytic theory of endemic misogyny. A fair criticism by conservative readers was my off-handed dismissal of their grievances against Hillary as minor compared with my speculation about a virulent unconscious misogyny that affected their judgment against her. I also neglected to mention possible non-psychoanalytic causes of misogyny, such as anatomical differences like the generally greater physical strength of men, which, in the traditional division of labor, enabled them to be the breadwinner, to hunt and protect the family, while women, who were generally more emotionally oriented and nurturing, gave birth to children and raised them, cooked and tended the household. However, with the sociocultural progress of modern life, these differences have become relatively moot, with women now equally capable of being strong breadwinners, and men capable of nurturing and raising children.

Notwithstanding this ostensible gender parity, misogyny continues to prevail. This is possibly due to a residual of biologically based discrimination, but I would argue that the main culprits are the psychodynamic antecedents of endemic misogyny discussed in the article.

In spite of the animosity against Hillary, she won the popular vote by approximately three million votes. If she had been more personable, warm, charismatic and less defensive, she might not have triggered so much hatred, and might have defeated Trump handily. Hillary's greatest accomplishment in the 2016 election was to demonstrate that America was ready to elect a female president.

Chapter VI **|**

THE POLITICAL ALLURE OF BEING "ABOVE THE LAW"

1. All Our Children: The Inner Appeal of America's
   Primal Families *(Los Angeles Times,* 2001)
2. The Politics of Confession *(Los Angeles Times,* 2001)
3. The Politics of Narcissism: America's Grandiose Persona
   Under Bush *(CounterPunch,* 2004)

When the Clintons were leaving the White House and *The Sopranos* was starting its second season on HBO, I published my first piece on the narcissistic allure of being "above the law" in the *Los Angeles Times* (March 18, 2001). At this time, the Clintons and the Sopranos were America's most riveting families. I explained the human psychological appeal of acting above the law by using Freud's 1914 paper, "On Narcissism." Ironically, in the first piece I wrote about Donald Trump ("Trumping Americans: The Strange, Irresistible Appeal of a Narcissistic Bloviator," page 154), I employed similar psychodynamic explanations. This is the Clintons/Sopranos piece.

All Our Children:
The Inner Appeal of America's Primal Families

SECTION M **OPINION** Los Angeles Times
SUNDAY March 18, 2001

All Our Children: The Inner Appeal of America's Primal Families

Return of the repressed: James Gandolfini and Edie Falco of "The Sopranos," left; Hillary Clinton and Bill Clinton, right.

▶ PSYCHOLOGY

By Peter Wolson

Why are the Sopranos and the Clintons America's most riveting families? The beginning of President George W. Bush's administration and the stock-market nose dive have been all but eclipsed by the public's fascination with the long-anticipated return of TV's fictional Mafia family, the Sopranos, and the daily revelations of "sleazy transgressions" by the Clintons during their last days in the White House.

Is there a correlation between the Sopranos' and Clintons' voyeuristic appeal? Could it be explained by the stimulation of some common psychological dynamic in the American psyche that makes these families irresistible to watch?

Psychologically, the Sopranos and Clintons are exceptionally user-friendly. The public can easily identify with an upper-middle-class New Jersey family living in the suburbs—the Sopranos—and with a middle-class Arkansas family—the Clintons—who achieved the American dream of becoming the nation's first family. But what makes these two families so enticing is that when they act, it's as if the ethics, morality and laws of society don't apply to them. The public is both repulsed and fascinated when these family members can impulsively do whatever they want at society's expense and not be burdened by a conscience.

What's so intriguing about people who break social rules and don't care about hurting others?

Sigmund Freud theorized that human beings begin life totally self-absorbed. Infants lack the cognitive and perceptual capacities to distinguish themselves from

"Why are the Sopranos and the Clintons America's most riveting families? The beginning of President George W. Bush's administration and the stock market nose dive have been all but eclipsed by the public's fascination with the long-anticipated return of TV's fictional Mafia family, the Sopranos, and the daily revelations of "sleazy transgressions" by the Clintons during their last days in the White House.

Is there a correlation between the Sopranos' and Clintons' voyeuristic appeal? Could it be explained by the stimulation of some common psychological dynamic in the American psyche that makes these families irresistible to watch?

Psychologically, the Sopranos and Clintons are exceptionally user-friendly. The public can easily identify with an upper-middle-class New Jersey family living in the suburbs—the Sopranos—and with a middle-class Arkansas family—the Clintons—who achieved the American dream of becoming the nation's first family. But what makes these two families so enticing is that when they act, it's as if the ethics, morality and laws of society don't apply to them. The public is both repulsed and fascinated when these family members can impulsively do whatever they want at society's expense and not be burdened by a conscience.

What's so intriguing about people who break social rules and don't care about hurting others?

Sigmund Freud theorized that human beings begin life as totally self-absorbed. Infants lack the cognitive and perceptual capacities to distinguish themselves from the outside world. Nothing exists apart from themselves. They begin life feeling omnipotent. They are motivated by their immediate impulses and exploitatively use their parents to fulfill their needs. When frustrated, they become enraged and want to destroy the source of frustration.

Through parental discipline, socialization and psychological maturation, children gradually learn that they are not omnipotent, that they need to depend on others for vital caretaking. Parents help them respect others, modulate their aggression and differentiate right from wrong. But, according to Freud, we all pay a heavy psychological toll for repressing our infantile narcissistic longings. We lose a type of paradise in which we felt that the world was our oyster, in which we could demand the satisfaction of our immediate needs and wreak the most horrific vengeance, in fantasy, against those who defy us. Throughout life we are burdened by constantly having to suppress these unconscious, primitive impulses.

Freud speculated that we are intrigued by criminals and jungle cats because they freely pursue the fulfillment of their predatory impulses. By identifying with them, we gratify infantile narcissistic wishes. Similarly, that's why we love Western gunfights, Nazi dramas and rogue cops like Dirty Harry. As we watch Mafia chief Tony Soprano ordering his henchmen to dispose of Richie, his prospective brother-in-law, after Tony's sister has murdered him, and imagine Clinton having sex with Monica or pardoning fugitive financier Marc Rich putatively in exchange for contributions to the Clinton library, we are repulsed. But, unconsciously, we re-experience the heady days of infancy when we were omnipotent and, in fantasy, could obtain satisfaction and express aggression unrestricted by social rules.

Ironically, even when Tony Soprano seeks therapy to overcome his anxiety attacks triggered by guilt over his murderous impulses, he wants it to help him become a better criminal. Similarly, Clinton dodges therapy for his adulterous behavior by soliciting spiritual guidance from a reverend who is an adulterer as well. Both Hillary Rodham Clinton and Carmela Soprano, Tony's wife, turn a blind eye to their husbands' antisocial activities while personally profiting from them.

Paradoxically, being repulsed by these families makes it possible to be fascinated by them. By disowning our infantile narcissistic desires and projecting them onto the Sopranos and Clintons, we can believe that we are more decent than they while unconsciously identifying with their transgressions.

Yet, the public's revulsion toward the Clintons has increased since they left the White House. Americans, including many Democrats, seem to loathe Clinton's pardons and commutations even more than the Sopranos' criminal behavior. But are ostensibly self-serving pardons more offensive than illicit campaign contributions and having oral sex with Monica while making war in the Balkans?

It appears that as long as Clinton was president, Americans could forgive his trespasses. Like Zeus, he could commit adultery, and the public would identify with his omnipotence and focus on his accomplishments. But when he left office, and Americans can no longer idealize him as a powerful figure, he and his family were devalued.

Nonetheless, the Clintons, like the Sopranos, remain irresistibly fascinating. Americans eagerly wait to see how the Sopranos will criminally cope with the frustrations of suburban living and what new dirt will be unearthed about Bill, Hillary, Roger and Hugh. But they might be surprised to realize that their irreverent excitement and contemptuous pleasure is largely derived from re-experiencing an infantile, self-centered, predatory part of themselves."

Commentary: Clearly, the public's perception of the Clintons' acting "above the law" stigmatized and undermined their attempt to return to the White House in the 2016 presidential election, this time with Hillary running for POTUS and Bill for First Gentleman. Republicans and even FBI director James Comey severely criticized Hillary for her "careless" use of her personal email server, which had exposed confidential, top-secret government business to potential hackers. Trump capitalized on the public perception of Hillary's moral corruption by encouraging his supporters at campaign rallies to shout "Lock her up!" and he encouraged Russian hackers to find more "dirt" on her private use of emails, ostensibly not caring if such encouragement was illegal and an unethical collaboration with a foreign power.

Republicans lambasted Hillary further for exploiting her role as

Secretary of State during the Obama administration to obtain huge fees for speeches to Wall Street bankers. Critics portrayed the Clintons as Arkansas white trash, using their political power to become wealthy at the expense of the American people. Trump and Republicans in the 2016 campaign emphasized Bill's sexual scandals and presidential impeachment to tarnish the Clintons' image as morally corrupt. They called attention to Bill's peccadillos to divert attention from Trump's misogynistic sexual "boys' talk" with Billy Bush that had gone viral.

Thus in the 2016 campaign, there was ample evidence from Trump and the Clintons of acting above the law in the service of narcissistic exploitation. In the paper "Political Power: An Alluring Stimulus for Regression and Omnipotence" (2009), I explore this narcissistic psychodynamic in further detail.

During Bill Clinton's Monica Lewinsky scandal, he redeemed himself with the American people by confessing that he "did have sex with that woman," revoking his original denial. Ironically, a number of his most vicious, sanctimonious Republican critics, including Gary Condit, Newt Gingrich and Henry Hyde had committed the same immoral sexual violations in political office, another poignant example of projective identification: disowning, displacing and projecting one's own problems into an "other."

California Congressman Gary Condit, known as a god-fearing Christian family-man, repeatedly denied his affair with the missing Chandra Levy, who was later found murdered. This ruined Condit's political reputation. It seemed that if he had been more forthright and accepted responsibility, he might have improved his chances of a more favorable political future. His denial inspired me to write an op-ed for the *Los Angeles Times* about the psychological dynamics of political confession. It was published on September 2, 2001.

The Politics of Confession

"In our media-driven society, is a politician's confession of transgression designed simply to gratify America's appetite for salacious theater and to protect the politician's self-interests? Or does it express a meaningful, human connection between the public and its elected representatives?

The customarily scripted expressions of remorse, coupled with the public's voyeuristic excitement over possible revelations of sexual details, has led to the widespread belief that political confessions, like former

President Bill Clinton's and what was expected of Rep. Gary A. Condit (D-Ceres), are all show and no substance. They can ruin or save a politician's career, but because of their self-serving, theatrical nature, one can barely tell if they also reflect a caring, responsible relationship between the politician and his constituency.

If these confessions are merely libidinal theater, why do the media and the public demand them from transgressing politicians? What needs do they fulfill in America's psyche?

The most pressing need is for a believable expression of guilt and remorse for the harm the politician has perpetrated against his constituency and others. Assuming responsibility for hurting others is the *sine qua non* of caring for one's fellow human beings. Politicians are elected as our political and moral leaders. They represent America's conscience, like our parents. If a politician is incapable of showing remorse for a betrayal of the public trust, as was initially the case for Clinton—"I did not have sex with that woman!"—and, more recently, for Condit, who has expressed no guilt over his putative affair with the missing Chandra Levy, the public cannot forgive him for his trespasses. He is judged as too self-serving and narcissistic to deserve office.

Even though they know these confessions are often well-rehearsed, Americans require the political confession to determine if the politician is capable of caring for his constituency and upholding an appropriate moral standard. Americans look very closely for "believable" expressions of guilt and remorse, to see whether the politician is willing to accept responsibility for betraying them.

However, the politician is in a highly precarious position. He knows that if he confesses his political "sins" too openly, his reputation can be ruined instantly. This probably motivated Clinton to initially deny his affair with Monica S. Lewinsky and Condit to "stonewall" about Levy.

The electorate's need for appropriate repentance and redemption often competes with its need to sully the politician's reputation out of envy. This is because leaders inevitably arouse envy in their followers, who desire their power, success and money. As an assemblyman and congressman who built his reputation on being a model of Christian propriety—he was one of the first to condemn Clinton for his infidelity— Condit became a perfect candidate for envious attacks. When his infidelity with Levy was revealed, the media and the public derived great pleasure from turning the tables on him. However, his fatal flaw was in not expressing appropriate remorse.

By revealing the weaknesses of their political leaders, public confessions allow Americans to reduce their envy through triumphant devaluations. While envious attacks can potentially destroy good politicians, like Sen. Edmund S. Muskie, the exposure of a politician's weaknesses may have the positive effect of making idealized political leaders appear more human and accessible.

Moreover, the political exposure of infidelity frequently threatens other politicians, who are inclined to disown and project their own infidelity onto the vulnerable confessor. Among Clinton's most vicious attackers were politicians like Condit, Rep. Henry J. Hyde and former House Speaker Newt Gingrich, all of whom had committed infidelities themselves. They scapegoated him for their own boundary violations.

Perhaps the most shocking function of the political confession is providing sexual material for voyeuristic gratification. The American public eagerly awaited details of Condit's affair with Levy. For many commentators, his refusal to admit the affair, let alone provide salacious sexual gossip, was the most disappointing aspect of his prime-time interview with Connie Chung. Unlike independent counsel Kenneth W. Starr, whose graphic report on Clinton's and Lewinsky's sexual affair entertained Americans for months, Condit refused to let the public into his bedroom. This merely fueled the public's frustration with him.

It is no wonder that politicians have to be very careful about how they reveal themselves. After the Nixon–Kennedy debates, in which Richard

M. Nixon's refusal to wear make-up may have cost him the 1960 presidential election, politicians have hired consultants to orchestrate their every move, especially when they are forced to give a public confession.

The political confession is pervasively flawed. It provides ammunition for envious attacks on politicians. It arouses and gratifies the public's prurient, voyeuristic interests, and it motivates politicians to turn to theatrical performances to salvage their careers. Yet, to the extent that it allows the public to evaluate whether the transgressor is truly remorseful for betraying the public trust, even if the confession is theatrically staged, it remains one of the best litmus tests for determining a politician's capacity to accept responsibility and care for his constituents."

Commentary: The issue of political confession highlights the conflict between narcissism and object relatedness, the preservation of the politician's reputation and political self-esteem versus the capacity to take responsibility for one's moral failures and correct them in the interest of one's constituency. Denying errors of judgment makes the politician appear to be self-serving and defensive, and it engenders distrust. We raise our children to accept responsibility for their mistakes as a reflection of good character and moral integrity. But confessing moral failures also risks destroying the public trust in a politician and can ruin his or her reputation. In addition, we must consider the public's envy of people in power and their *schadenfreude*, their pleasure in defeating them.

Hillary Clinton initially denied her culpability in (while Secretary of State) using a personal email server that included top-secret documents requiring a security clearance. She defended her use of a personal email server by citing Colin Powell, who also employed a private server. But his didn't contain classified emails because he didn't conduct government business on it. Even after surviving an eleven-hour Senatorial investigation over her role in the Benghazi crisis, she continued to be perceived as defensively acting "above the law." It would have helped her to be forthright and to admit her failures of judgment rather than making excuses for them. In general, if she had been more open about her Wall Street speeches, her participation in the Benghazi situation and her emails, she would have appeared less guarded and would have provoked less antipathy.

In contrast, Donald Trump lost the popular vote but confesses nothing and accepts no responsibility for his inconsistency or unfulfilled promises. He never admits shame or guilt yet remains exceptionally popular among his base. Would he have won the popular vote if he had displayed a more mature, responsible attitude? Possibly. However, he won the presidency through lying, insulting, fomenting racism, and being sexually and aggressively scabrous, and still had the support of the Catholic Church, Evangelicals and respected, intelligent conservative Republicans. This suggests that the moral fiber of America has deteriorated. I discuss this more thoroughly later.

Lord Acton was correct. Power has corrupted the American political and religious establishment, and this psychological degradation must be exposed in order to fight and repair it. As the most successful, powerful democracy that has ever existed, we are possibly witnessing America's decline through psychological regression and moral decay. However, in my piece, "America's White-Lash and the Degradation of Reason" (see page 165), I attributed this decline to the unconscious threat of our country's growing multiculturalism and diversity to the hegemony of America's traditional white male culture. I predicted that America's recovery from this regression will materialize gradually in the increasing acceptance and embracing of "otherness," especially as cultural diversity becomes the American way of life.

Narcissistic dynamics were abundantly represented in the presidential administration of George W. Bush (2001 to 2009), particularly in his foreign and military policies. His administration's distrust of the United Nations and foreign countries along with its neocon war strategy of unilateral preemption, were major symptoms of a narcissistic mentality, and prompted me to write this piece for *CounterPunch*, published on February 14, 2004:

The Politics of Narcissism:
America's Grandiose Persona Under Bush

"As the death toll of American soldiers rises daily in Iraq, Democratic presidential contenders are attacking President Bush's policy of unilateral preemption and urging him to share post-war responsibilities with the international community. But the Bush administration appears reluctant to relinquish control. Instead, while aggrandizing American superiority and pursuing a policy of global intimidation, it has been displaying contempt for international collaboration and trumpeting its isolationism. Under the Bush presidency, could it be that the face of America has begun to look like a narcissistic personality disorder?

What are the traits of this syndrome? How have they been reflected in the Bush administration, and what are their implications for the 2004 presidential election?

A display of grandiosity and superiority

A narcissistic display of grandiosity usually compensates for a sense of vulnerability and helplessness. Clearly, 9/11 made Americans feel extremely vulnerable and, consequently, willing to accept President Bush's grandiose policy of unilateral preemption without much protest. As outlined by neocons Richard Perl and Secretary of Defense Paul Wolfowitz years before 9/11, this strategy expresses the superior attitude that the United States, as the most powerful country on earth, has the right to forcibly remove the leaders of other nations who are judged to pose a threat to American security, and impose its democratic form of government upon them. As President Bush recently told Tim Russert on *Meet the Press*, he reserves the right to wage war to achieve these goals without having to consult with the international community.

Arrogantly, President Bush railed against the slow pace at which the United Nations conducted its search for Saddam's weapons of mass destruction (WMDs), ignored protests from the international community and proceeded to attack Iraq. Since the war, he has been accused by domestic and international critics alike of engaging in American imperialism, and the rationale for the war is now under intense scrutiny.

Grandiosity was also reflected in the Bush administration's mistaken belief that the Iraqis, after thousands of years of living under authoritarian governance, would heartily welcome the American liberators and the chance to establish a democracy. Instead, American soldiers were generally greeted with resentment and daily homicidal terrorist attacks. The anticipation of a joyous welcome was a narcissistic projection of the Bush administration's idealized, egocentric belief system and reflected a lack of empathy for a different culture.

A profound distrust and avoidance of dependency often accompanied by contempt for others

A narcissistic personality fears that dependency poses the threat of feeling weak, humiliated and dominated by the other. In an increasingly interdependent socioeconomic world, the Bush administration seems to fear that involvement with other countries places the United States in a position to be controlled and exploited by them. Its contempt for participation in the United Nations and even in NATO is used to defend America against this vulnerable, dependent position.

A conviction that it is "a dog-eat-dog world," one can only trust one's self, and a predilection for "splendid isolation."

Since dependency is psychologically dangerous, the only one the narcissist can trust is himself. The Bush administration seems to believe that the United States can only rely upon itself. The guiding principle of unilateral preemption is: "Do unto others before they can do unto you." Thus, the rationale for President Bush's preemptive attack against an "imminently threatening" Saddam Hussein.

Ironically, after 9/11 there was an outpouring of empathy for the United States from France, Germany and the world community at large. But instead of capitalizing on this international support, the Bush administration's distrust of others has led to a detachment from other nations.

The grandiose idealization of "going it alone" certainly appeals to the masculine Western tradition of America's rugged individualism. But when taken to the extreme of a lone gunslinger—fighting the "evildo-ers" who are "wanted dead or alive"—it smacks of defensive grandiosity. As a result of its isolationism, the Bush administration now has to face the responsibility of American soldiers dying daily from terrorist attacks with few international troops to relieve this tragic burden.

A dominating, exploitative use of others, and an inclination to use or ignore the law as it suits one's own purposes

It appears that the Bush administration will engage with other nations only when it is dominant and able to use them for self-serving needs. Thus, it is willing to ask other countries for soldiers and equipment, as long as it can retain control of Iraq rather than share decision-making power in Iraq's rebuilding. This is in contrast to a more mature form of international collaboration in which giving and taking among nations is on an egalitarian, mutually respectful basis. Recently asking the United Nations for help with Iraq's elections is far too little, too late.

As for observing the law, the Bush administration ignored the UN's mandate to continue looking for weapons of mass destruction before using force, by preemptively attacking Iraq. Yet it was critical of leaders, like Saddam Hussein, who defied UN mandates.

Moreover, it justified the war as necessary to safeguard the United States against Saddam's alleged WMDs, although these have not been found. Increasingly, it appears that the president deceptively used this rationale to attack Iraq for other reasons, as suggested by former Bush

Treasury Secretary Paul O'Neill, who also accused the administration of lying. In addition, awarding lucrative contracts to firms, like Halliburton, with which both the Bush family and Vice President Cheney have been intimately involved, raises questions of self-serving exploitation.

A reliance upon revenge in retaliation for injuries to self-esteem.

Various pundits have speculated that that the administration's leak of the CIA identity of Ambassador Joseph Wilson's wife, Valerie Plame, as well as the Treasury Department's investigation of Paul O'Neill immediately following his *60 Minutes* interview, were acts of revenge for their embarrassing disclosures against the Bush administration.

Others have conjectured that the war against Iraq was mainly an act of revenge for Saddam's assassination attempt against the first President Bush. Thus, President Bush's administration, with its America *uber alles* superiority, has increasingly insulted and alienated America's allies. This has fostered a hostile international climate that has made these countries reluctant to help us and may eventually breed more terrorism. With so many issues at stake in the 2004 presidential election, the one that influences all the rest is whether we want the face of America to look like a bully masking vulnerability through exploitative domination. In light of the United States' sense of vulnerability since 9/11 and President Bush's popularity, could this intimidating, grandiose persona be America's new ideal?"

Commentary: George W. Bush's psychologically regressed narcissistic administration prevailed for four more years, and it wasn't until President Barack Obama's administration in 2009 that America restored a more mature, egalitarian ethos of collaboration, respect and concern for others in international and domestic relations.

Donald Trump's presidential victory in 2016 signified a regression to narcissism, only worse than under Bush. The narcissistic parallels are immediately evident: "America *(uber alles)* first," distrust of international collaboration, the fear of other countries exploiting us in trade deals

(NAFTA, TPP, etc.), "splendid isolation," the need to get revenge against perceived enemies, and authoritarian bullying. This might, in part, be due to the fact that the mental health of the American population had regressed from neurotic problems of inhibition to narcissistic problems of impulsivity and aggression. This is discussed in the next section.

Chapter VII |

ANALYZING SOCIETAL VIOLENCE, CRIMINALITY AND ITS PSYCHOLOGICAL AFTERMATH

1. Strange to Say, but Neurotics Are Preferable
    (Los Angeles Times, 1999)

2. The Aurora Massacre: Coping With The Precariousness Of Human Existence *(Huffington Post, 2012)*

3. The Joe Paterno Syndrome: Idealization and the Corruption of Morality *(Huffington Post, 2011)*

At the time of publishing the next piece in the *Los Angeles Times* on August 22, 1999, outbreaks of violence were occurring everywhere in America, and a palpable fear pervaded the country, unlike anything in my lifetime. In this article, I attempted to account for America's societal breakdown by focusing on the regression in the psychological diagnoses of the American population. Most people in the past suffered from neurotic problems of inhibition brought on by excessive guilt. With the breakdown of the nuclear family and the prevalence of divorce, childhood neglect, abandonment and abuse, by 1999, primitive disorders of impulsivity, drug addiction, sexual abuse, narcissistic conditions, and borderline and schizoid problems prevailed. People no longer had sufficient control over their aggressive impulses, and violence appeared to be cracking the thin veneer of American civilization. This is the piece.

Strange to Say, but Neurotics Are Preferable

"The recent outbreak of mass violence in Atlanta and Los Angeles, after the carnage at Columbine High School in Littleton, Colorado, has shocked and frightened Americans into wondering what has broken down in our society. Still, it is remarkable how well psychological regulators of aggression have worked in the United States, a largely free and open society. While it is appropriate to account for the apparent erosion of social controls, it is equally important to ask how we have been so effective in containing violence.

According to Sigmund Freud, human beings are animals motivated primarily by their sexual and aggressive impulses. In his *Civilization and Its Discontents*, the psychoanalyst argued that civilization, through principles of morality, law and order and social propriety, controls human aggression to protect us from each other. These learned regulators, however, do not guarantee that our basic animal nature will not rear its ugly head, particularly in a democracy in which aggression is widely tolerated. Nonetheless, mass murder in America is quite rare.

So what, if anything, has broken down in the American psyche?

Since the perpetrators of recent attacks have had severe psychological problems, perhaps part of the answer lies in the radical shift in the diagnosis of mental health patients since the 1960s, from inhibited neurosis to impulse-ridden and narcissistic disorders. Neurotics are overly controlled by strict consciences, right and wrong, and their fears of disapproval for expressing sexual and aggressive impulses.

Through the guilt-ridden 1950s, the American nuclear family was the primary emissary of society's moral values. Outbreaks of violence were largely confined to an isolated murder here and there. In the '60s, the rising divorce rate undercut the nuclear family. American values embraced the freedom to pursue pleasure—sexual, drug-induced, etc. Guilt became bad, impulsivity good.

From the late '60s till now, therapists have noticed that their patients no longer mainly suffer from inhibition and guilt. Instead, impulse disorders, drug and sexual addictions, eating disorders and victims of sexual and physical abuse have proliferated. These patients are much more difficult to treat than neurotics. They tend to be extremely egocentric and infantile, filled with aggression and possessing little empathic sensitivity toward their fellow man.

Their family histories are strewn with parental neglect, abandonment and abuse. Many come from broken homes and thus lack the regulatory experience of a united parental couple whose moral standards they can emulate and internalize.

A flagrant absence of guilt and a lack of empathic sensitivity were certainly evident in the minds of Buford O. Furrow Jr., who confessed to wounding five at a Jewish community center in Granada Hills and to slaying a postal worker, and Mark O. Barton, a day trader in Atlanta who killed 12, including his family, before taking his own life. For these killings, the primary psychological mechanism was projective identification. Furrow had a history of job problems and a failed marriage to the ex-wife of a founder of the racist group the Order, and who had threatened to kill

her and himself, displaced his homicidal impulses onto Jews: By identifying with the racially superior Aryan Nations, he compensated for his
inferior self-image, which he then projected into Jews. In trying to kill
Jews, Furrow was attempting to kill off the hated, disowned parts of himself. Similarly, Barton's slaying of day traders whom he described as out
to "greedily destroy" him, was an effort to kill his own greedy, destructive
impulses that were causing him so much anguish.

Projective identification is a powerful instrument for the discharge
of murderous rage since it involves the denial of victims' separate existence, thereby eliminating the possibility of empathizing with another
person. Accordingly, the perpetrator can freely use the victim for his or
her own exploitative homicidal purposes without being impeded by guilt
or remorse.

But do these individual murderous acts highlight a more general
breakdown of the regulators that society uses to control aggression? The
overwhelming majority of mental patients are not violent. They are more
likely to be withdrawn and fearful than to attack others, as indicated
by the behavior of the insane homeless on our streets. Our extreme fear
and panic over the shootings in Granada Hills and Atlanta may have
been due to our lack of preparation for such violent outbreaks precisely
because they are so infrequent.

Some have contended that the media, because of television's immediate, unrelenting coverage of violent events and the Internet instigate
copy-cat killings or may even help potential perpetrators procure and
use lethal weapons. On the other hand, saturation coverage incidentally
informs the public how to best protect itself. In this sense, the media
serves the function of a ubiquitous, societal superego, monitoring our
lives for potential threats. For example, as a result of the public being
informed about recent shootings, there has been a crescendo of calls
for tougher gun control, for stronger standards of propriety and more
empathic sensitivity to isolated loners.

It is fascinating to note that after Furrow's rampage, the conversations among hate-group members over the Internet were extremely divided, with a majority of participants critical of Furrow's action, not from a sense of conscience but from the standpoint of reason. Many thought his actions were self-defeating and likely to provoke a backlash against their group. This open, diverse exchange, made possible by the Internet, may modulate the more violent members of these groups.

In addition, superego controls have been strengthened through a resurgence of interest in religion. Marriage is on the rise, and the divorce rate is declining, which may buttress moral values. In high-crime areas, community policing has increased. Unfortunately, since guilt no longer plays a prominent regulatory role in the American psyche, society must rely more on external controls than on internal ones.

We are responding in part to the challenge of a weakened moral fiber with a greater emphasis on family values and education. Nonetheless, even with its fissures, the thin veneer of American civilization is thicker than one might think."

Commentary: Certainly, in clinical practice, psychotherapists are concerned about the primitiveness of the patient population. We often complain about how rare it is to treat a neurotic patient who has problems of inhibition. Effective psychoanalysis and psychoanalytic therapy free patients from defensive self-constraints so they can embrace and exhibit who they are, warts and all, without debilitating shame, guilt or neurotic symptoms. In treating pre-Oedipal narcissistic, borderline, impulse disorders and traumatic dissociative states, the therapeutic task often has to do with taming aggression through the development of adaptive defensive structures. These primitive patients need to strengthen their egos and superegos in order to use appropriate guilt and shame to modulate their aggression and boundary violations. It is much more difficult to develop and build internal defensive structures in primitive patients than it is to resolve neurotic internal conflicts through effective interpretations and other interventions.

This piece raises the question of whether the instant communication through smartphones and the Internet (1) reinforces a culture of unhealthy narcissism, with Facebook, Instagram, Twitter and endless "selfies" or (2) promotes a more aggressive, mob mentality, like the cyberbullying of children in elementary and high school. Or is digital communication more helpful in times of crises, like hurricanes and fires, and for alerting authorities about criminal behavior?

Clearly, cyber-communication is neither good nor bad, but can be used for psychologically healthy or unhealthy purposes. Even considering the increasingly regressed psychological diagnoses of Americans, our overall physical safety appears to be quite secure, with few incidents of terrorism and crime, relative to the large size of our population. In fact, the national violent crime rate has decreased while the prevalence of mass murders has spiked.

Similarly, I wrote the next piece, which was published in the *Huffington Post* on July 31, 2012, in response to the mass slaying perpetrated by James Holmes in a movie theater in Aurora, Colorado. This piece highlighted the tentative, precarious nature of human existence and focused on gun control.

The Aurora Massacre: Coping With the Precariousness of Human Existence

"The Aurora massacre has provoked fears of life-threatening vulnerability and a desperate concern to prevent another mass slaying. Can a pragmatic solution be found? And if so, what? If not, how can we allay our existential fears?

Since the massacre, pundits have been arguing whether the government should encourage the public to detect and report to the authorities individuals exhibiting unusual changes in behavior, suggesting symptoms of mental illness, or should there be new laws passed to restrict the purchase of guns?

Most conservative pundits have decried the renewed focus on gun control, maintaining that "guns don't kill people, people kill people." They argue that even with more gun control legislation, a deranged individual intent on shooting innocent citizens, will find a way to obtain the guns. They insist that the Second Amendment to the United States Constitution guarantees the right of every American to bear arms in order to defend the right to life, liberty and the pursuit of happiness, especially to protect one's home and loved ones. One governor went so far as to say that it was unfortunate there weren't other armed citizens in the Aurora movie theater who could have shot the killer and stopped him. Others argued that in the dark theater, this might have caused more murders and mayhem.

Common sense tells us that restricting access to high-powered guns, capable of firing hundreds of rounds in seconds, would diminish the potential for mass murder. Enraged, crazed individuals are often addictively compelled to express violence. Controlling access to guns would make it more difficult for them to implement their barbaric fantasies. However, Larry Elder, a libertarian radio talk-show host, pointed out that some societies, like Canada's, which have easy access to guns, have fewer incidents of mass violence than the United States. He concluded that the culprit was cultural influence, not guns, and that ours is a more violent society.

Some pundits have focused on mental illness, rather than gun control. Unfortunately, predicting the potential for mass murder is virtually impossible. As a psychologist in clinical practice for 42 years, I have observed and treated all types of psychopathology in inpatient and outpatient settings, including psychotic patients with murderous fantasies, and none of them have murdered anyone, let alone committed mass murder. My experience is not unique. I don't know of any mental health professionals who can accurately predict the potential for mass murder in a given individual from symptoms of mental illness, unless they know that the person has acquired weapons, devised a specific plan and is extremely motivated to carry it out. If trained professionals cannot predict mass murder, how can one expect the police, family members or the public to do so? Moreover, the murder rate among schizophrenics is less than in the general population. The adoption of a nationwide mandate to report any signs of abnormal behavior to authorities would be tantamount to a witch-hunt and stigmatize the mentally ill more than they already are.

Pragmatically, the most we can do is be sensitive to explicit indications of danger in the present, such as seeing someone acting menacingly or carrying guns. This would be similar to the alertness for strange behavior in one's fellow passengers that air travelers have acquired since 9/11, for the purpose of identifying potential terrorists. However, even with such surveillance, the likelihood of preventing mass slayings, like Aurora's, is miniscule.

The sad truth is that regardless of what we do preventatively, we are virtually incapable of stopping massacres. "Shit happens!" Horrific events occur beyond our control, and there is little we can do about them. These events trigger existential anxiety and pervasive fears for our survival, derived from overwhelming feelings of vulnerability and helplessness. Many of us defend against this anxiety by reverting to fantasies of omnipotent control. Ironically, we often project our desire for omnipotent control into fantasy superhero saviors, like Batman, with whom we can identify, or, at times, even God. But Batman remains a fantasy, and God as most priests, rabbis and pastors would probably say,lends support and comfort but does not prevent catastrophes. In fact, catastrophes are explained as God's will. As illustrated in the Book of Job, God helps human beings accept catastrophes as unavoidable limitations of reality. Such acceptance is a prerequisite for moving on with their lives. Thus, he castigates Job for his omnipotent belief that being a good man, God's most loyal servant, should have prevented his life from being destroyed by Satan. When Job questions how God could have forsaken him, God answers: "How dare you question my will! I created the universe and everything in it." God admonishes Job for trying to omnipotently control him by being loyal and good. Job must ultimately accept that God, or reality, is more powerful than him, even when reality is unpredictable and destructive.

Thus, in the face of catastrophe, our healthiest psychological response is to mourn our unbearable losses and the losses of others and to have the humility to be aware of our helplessness and vulnerability. Our greatest challenge is to accept the unpredictable, uncertain nature of human existence, in which we and our loved ones might perish at any given moment. When confronted by tragedy, like Job and hopefully the Aurora massacre victims, we need to preserve the "audacity of hope" and our motivation to live vital, fulfilling lives."

Commentary: This piece obviously concerned gun control, the mentally ill, and the existential precariousness of life. "Americans are ten times more likely to be killed by guns than people in other high-income countries, a new study finds" (Robert Preidt, CBSnews.com, February 3,

2016). This report indicated that the firearm-related homicide rate in the US compared to 22 other high-income nations is 25 times higher. Yet, the passion for firearms is deeply ingrained in family traditions of hunting and shooting, and appears to be undeterred by catastrophic mass shootings, like the Aurora massacre or the mass killings of children at Sandy Hook school, in which twenty first graders and six school staff members were killed; the Pulse Orlando night club shooting in which 49 people were gunned to death; the Las Vegas rifle slaughter of 58 audience members at a country-western concert; and the Stoneman Douglas High School massacre in Parkland, Florida, in which 17 students and staff members were killed and 17 others were injured. These students have started a nationwide movement for gun control in lieu of the fact that politicians have failed to effectively address this problem.

Gun owners feel that possessing firearms makes them safer and believe that if other people in these massacres had been able to defend themselves with firearms, fewer killings would have occurred. Yet the freedom to carry prevailed in the "Wild West," which we had to curtail to make our citizens safer. Countries, like Japan, with the most stringent requirements to possess firearms, have relatively few gun deaths. Obviously, semi-automatic and fully automatic rifles facilitate mass killings. But Americans' love of shooting has made it virtually impossible to limit access to high-powered rifles.

The second issue of mentally deranged individuals, like James Holmes and Adam Lanza at Sandy Hook, is just as difficult to resolve. James Holmes was treated by a psychiatrist who knew that he was thinking of killing people three to four times a day at the time of the shooting, but could do nothing legally to place him on a psychiatric hold because he didn't disclose a specific plan. Adam Lanza was not receiving psychological treatment at the time of the Sandy Hook massacre, but had been evaluated previously in the ninth grade by the Yale University's Child Study Center. His mother refused to follow their recommendations for psychotropic medication and psychotherapy, and allowed him to possess and shoot firearms, including high-powered rifles with full-capacity magazines. He shot her to death before murdering the children at Sandy Hook elementary school. Americans need to understand that mental health practitioners cannot stop a mentally unstable person from committing murder unless the latter is willing to receive and respond positively to psychotherapy and psychotropic medication, and/or is sufficiently forthright to provide a legal basis for restraint.

The primary focus of this article is the difficulty of coping with the ever-present uncertainty of human existence. It is rare to know when or how we will die. It can happen at any moment and in any place. Often there is little we can do to prevent it. Attending a movie theater or elementary school would normally be considered safe. But the domestic terrorism of James Holmes and Adam Lanza, although expectable in hindsight, was unpredictable and unpreventable with our current gun laws. No matter how cautious we are, even living in a bomb shelter, we cannot prevent ourselves from dying from some unexpected cause.

Psychologically, it is important to acknowledge and respect our existential vulnerability while perhaps using it to our advantage as, the Cavalier poets of old and contemporary existentialists have exhorted us to do. "Live for today, for tomorrow we die!"

The next article describes a different type of societal aggression: how Joe Paterno, a beloved football coach at Penn State, was so adored by his students that they denied his complicity in allowing Jerry Sandusky, his assistant coach, to continue molesting children. Published in *The Huffington Post* on November 10, 2011, this blog illustrated how merging with an idealized leader can lead to a catastrophic loss of moral judgment. An HBO movie, starring Al Pacino as Joe Paterno, has recently aired. This piece was one of my more popular *Huffington Post* blogs, receiving a large number of responses from college students.

The Joe Paterno Syndrome:
Idealization and the Corruption of Morality

"On the evening of November 9th, 2011, more than a thousand of Penn State college students are vehemently protesting the firing of their beloved hero, Joe Paterno, the legendary football couch of Penn State, for not reporting to the police in 2002 his knowledge of coach Jerry Sandusky raping and sodomizing a ten-year-old boy in an athletic facility. Instead, Paterno merely passed the information on to school administrators, allegedly because Sandusky was already retired. The administrators punished Sandusky by depriving him of keys to the university locker room but left him with access to a university office, to young men at Penn State and to boys in the vicinity. Like Paterno, neither the administrators nor Penn State President, Graham Spanier, reported this incident to the police, which left Sandusky free to continue molesting children. In response to the public outcry over charges that Sandusky sexually corrupted eight children and to rectify these horrific lapses in moral judgment, the Board fired the President and Paterno. But the protesting students didn't seem to care about Paterno's moral lapse. They were protesting the Board's injustice to Paterno. His sin of omission, allowing a child molester to continue molesting, paled in comparison to losing their beloved football idol.

Unfortunately, this is quite common. Loving or caring about someone frequently blinds one to their trespasses. One is inclined to see them as all good, and to deny their faults in order to preserve one's idealization of them. Women who love their incestuous, child-molesting husbands or boyfriends frequently protect them to the detriment of their victimized children. Molested children often blame themselves for the molestations and deny the culpability of their molesters, in order to preserve what feels like a vital tie to their sadistic love objects.

Idealization serves a vital psychological need. Children idealize their parents as mentors to provide them with guidance and as models to emulate in order to identify and define their values, morality, direction and life goals. A major danger of idealization is merging with the idealized object and losing one's independent mind and moral judgment, like the cult followers of Jim Jones who drank the poisonous "Kool-Aid" under his messianic direction. Or like the devotees of Joseph Stalin who loved him even after he imprisoned and tortured them. Or like the Germans under Adolf Hitler while he committed the most unspeakable, barbaric crimes in the name of Aryan superiority.

Joe Paterno was an idealized father figure, a loving, strong protective model for his young football players and Penn State students to learn from and emulate. Unfortunately, he failed to follow his own advice to maintain civility, which he said was sorely lacking in today's society, by protecting his own students and young boys in the community from someone he knew to be a sexual predator.

With his lapse in moral judgment, he joins a prestigious group of Catholic priests, including Cardinal Roger Mahoney and even the Pope, who in the name of protecting their fellow clergymen and the reputation of the church, exposed hundreds of young boys and girls to sexual abuse by allowing child molesting priests to remain in contact with them. It obviously takes enormous strength, even from the most religious, god-fearing individuals, to prioritize one's own moral integrity over one's inclination to protect colleagues, friends, lovers and especially family members who have committed child abuse. No wonder it is so hard for the Penn State student protestors to see how their beloved father figure, Joe Paterno, failed to protect them in a most fundamental way."

Commentary: As this piece explained, idealization of parents and other caring adults is necessary for the internalization of a child's direction and goals in life, and ultimately helps consolidate a strong, cohesive sense of self (Kohut, 1977). However, it has a dark side, a primitive form of splitting, in which the idealized figure, such as a parent or a beloved coach, is perceived as infallible and all-good, even when he does something bad. To acknowledge anything wrong about an idealized father figure can make you feel guilty, like you have betrayed someone you love.

Many new psychotherapy patients feel such guilt about revealing disappointments and angry thoughts or feelings about their parents. Such denial undermines their capacity to acknowledge the harmful way their parents might have treated them. This prevents them from voicing their deepest concerns in order to resolve them in psychotherapy.

As noted earlier, adolescents typically rebel against and de-idealize their parents. This helps them to separate and individuate and to consolidate their own distinctive identity on their trajectory toward becoming independent, self-reliant adults. In the piece "When Politics Is Also Psychology" (see Wolson, page 56), both presidential candidates, Al Gore and George W. Bush, faced the challenge of separating and individuating from their powerful fathers in childhood. This arguably influenced their capacity to be strong, independent leaders. This dynamic also seemed to apply to Jeb Bush in his campaign for the Republican presidential nomination, which I described in "The Bush Boys: No Sibling Rivalry, but Maybe Something Deeper," for *Thomson Reuters* (see Wolson, page 63). This blog focused on Jeb's attempt to extricate himself from his dependency on the overshadowing influence of his older brother, George W., and the rest of his family. Clearly, mature psychological development requires a need to de-idealize one's internalized childhood love objects in order to establish one's own independent mind.

Chapter VIII

THE PSYCHOLOGY OF GENOCIDE AND TORTURE IN WAR

1. Politics of Victimhood: A Perpetual Cycle of Abuse
   (*Los Angeles Times*, 1999)

2. The Underlying Dynamic in Post-9/11 America: Exhibitionistic Revenge at Abu Ghraib (*CounterPunch*, 2004)

3. Compromising America's Integrity Versus Ensuring Military Security (*Huffington Post*, 2015)

Allison Silver asked me to write on the psychodynamics of Serbian pride related to their victimization by Albanian Muslims in their war over Kosovo. In this piece, I analyzed how the "pride of victimhood" among Christian Serbians fueled a culture of revenge. The piece was published in the *Los Angeles Times* on May 9, 1999.

Politics of Victimhood:
A Perpetual Cycle of Abuse

COMMENTARY / ANALYSIS / TIMES INTERVIEW

SECTION M

SUNDAY
MAY 9, 1999

OPINION

Los Angeles Times

POLITICS OF VICTIMHOOD

A Perpetual Cycle of Abuse

By Peter Wolson

When Serbs discuss their motivation to retain exclusive control over Kosovo, they recount a long, painful history of horrific victimization by foreign powers extending back to the Middle Ages. One would think that this history of national abuse would engender a feeling of humiliation in the Serbian psyche. But, on the contrary, Serbs typically display their victimhood with intense nationalistic pride. How can we explain this surprising correlation, and how does it relate to committing atrocities against ethnic Albanians?

Psychoanalytically, when a nation's collective psyche is wounded through humiliating military defeats and the abuse of its people, it is in danger of fragmentation and loss of identity. In order to survive, the national psyche must compensate for its devastated self-esteem by restoring its pride. The greater the narcissistic wound, the more defensively grandiose it must become, believing it is superior to other nations and sometimes even concluding its inhabitants are God's "chosen people." Mortifying national shame is unconsciously transformed into glorified victimhood associated with intense nationalistic fervor.

This psychodynamic has obviously been a powerful organizing principle for the Serbian people. Over the centuries,

Peter Wolson, a clinical psychologist, is director of training at the Los Angeles Institute and Society for Psychoanalytic Studies.

after being abused and subjected by Ottoman Turks, Albanian Muslims, Austrians and Nazis, the Serbs inflated their national pride with the belief that they were a "chosen people" of God. Yugoslav President Slobodan Milosevic rose to power vowing to avenge Serbia's wounds by returning their mystical Holy Land, Kosovo, to its people.

We see the same transformation from victimhood to grandiose collective pride in the Old Testament, where the Egyptian persecution of God's "chosen people," the ancient Israelites, is celebrated in the Passover Seder with the vow, "Never again."

Similarly, Germany's humiliation following the forced payment of excessive World War I reparations to its Western conquerors was transformed into a grandiose nationalistic triumph by Adolf Hitler, who proclaimed that the German people were a superior Aryan race.

Such psychological compensation for national victimhood is understandable, but how do "ethnic cleansing," genocide and other forms of abuse relate to this? One would think the last thing a victimized nation would do is victimize another, especially in the fashion it has been abused. But this does not hold true.

Psychologically, we know that adult victims of childhood physical and sexual abuse are inclined to perpetuate the same abuse with their children. This is because of a principle known as "identification with the aggressor." To protect himself, the abused individual unconsciously identifies with his victimizer and so seeks to

Please see ABUSE, M6

TIM TEEBKEN/For The Times

Abuse
Continued from M1

overcome the feeling of being abused. We see this psychological defense operating in victims of kidnapping, like Patty Hearst in 1974, who start to identify with their kidnappers.

The relationship between victim and victimizer is unconsciously internalized in the abused individual's psyche. This internalization also occurs in a nation's collective unconscious when it has experienced traumatic abuse. Nations overcome humiliation by defeating their enemies in the case of Serbia, the ethnic Muslim Albanians, their ancient nemesis.

The former victim seeks revenge by forcing the victimizer to experience the same abuse he perpetrated. Thus, the Serbs under Milosevic are repossessing their national spiritual home by subjecting ethnic Albanians to the same "ethnic cleansing" the latter perpetrated against them during the Middle Ages.

The problem with overcoming one's victimization by victimizing the abuser is that the cycle never ends. As long as the victim-victimizer dynamic exists in a nation's psyche, the nation will be unconsciously motivated to seek out other victimizers to triumph over.

This self-destructive cycle can only stop when the nation achieves a strong, stable and secure national identity. Thus, the Marshall Plan, which facilitated Germany's recovery after World War II, in contrast with the humiliating reparations of World War I, led to the development of a healthy, democratic German psyche.

NATO's policy of bombing Yugoslavia is likely to fuel the Serbs' nationalistic pride and determination to overcome another shameful defeat. The critical but perplexing question remains, how can the Serbs become geopolitically strong and secure enough to cut the pathological link between victimhood and national pride and end their need for a "victim-victimizer" psychology?

"When Serbs discuss their motivation to retain exclusive control over Kosovo, they recount a long, painful history of horrific victimization by foreign powers extending back to the Middle Ages. One would think that this history of national abuse would engender a feeling of humiliation in the Serbian psyche. But, on the contrary, Serbs typically display their victimhood with intense nationalistic pride. How can we explain this surprising correlation, and how does it relate to committing atrocities against ethnic Albanians?

Psychoanalytically, when a nation's collective psyche is wounded through humiliating military defeats and the abuse of its people, it is in danger of fragmentation and loss of identity. In order to survive, the national psyche must compensate for its devastated self-esteem by restoring its pride. The greater the narcissistic wound, the more defensively grandiose it must become, believing it is superior to other nations and sometimes even concluding that its inhabitants are God's "chosen people." Mortifying national shame is unconsciously transformed into glorified victimhood associated with intense nationalistic fervor.

This psychodynamic has obviously been a powerful organizing principle for the Serbian people. Over the centuries, after being abused and subjected by Ottoman Turks, Albanian Muslims, Austrians and Nazis, the Serbs inflated their national pride with the belief that they were a "chosen people" of God. Yugoslav President Slobodan Milošević rose to power vowing to avenge Serbia's wounds by returning their mystical Holy Land, Kosovo, to its people.

We see the same transformation from victimhood to grandiose collective pride in the Old Testament, where the Egyptian persecution of God's "chosen people," the ancient Israelites, is celebrated in the Passover Seder with the vow, "Never again." Similarly, Germany's humiliation following the forced payment of excessive World War I reparations to its Western conquerors was transformed into a grandiose nationalistic triumph by Adolf Hitler, who proclaimed that the German people were a superior Aryan race.

Such psychological compensation for national victimhood is understandable, but how do "ethnic cleansing," genocide and other forms of abuse relate to this? One would think the last thing a victimized nation would do is victimize another, especially in the fashion it has been abused. But this does not hold true.

Psychologically, we know that adult victims of childhood physical and sexual abuse are inclined to perpetuate the same abuse with their children. This is because of a principle known as "identification with the aggressor." To protect himself, the abused individual unconsciously identifies with his victimizer and so seeks to overcome the feeling of being abused. We see this psychological defense operating in victims of kidnapping, like Patty Hearst in 1979, who start to identify with their kidnappers.

The relationship between victim and victimizer is unconsciously internalized in the abused individual's psyche. This internalization also occurs in a nation's collective unconscious when it has experienced traumatic abuse. Nations overcome humiliation by defeating their enemies: in the case of Serbia, the ethnic Muslim Albanians, their ancient nemesis.

The former victim seeks revenge by forcing the victimizer to experience the same abuse he perpetrated. Thus, the Serbs under Milošević are repossessing their national spiritual home by subjecting ethnic Albanians to the same "ethnic cleansing" the latter perpetrated against them during the Middle Ages.

The problem with overcoming one's victimization by victimizing the abuser is that the cycle never ends. As long as the victim–victimizer dynamic exists in a nation's psyche, the nation will be unconsciously motivated to seek out other victimizers to triumph over.

This self-destructive cycle can only stop when the nation achieves a strong, stable and secure national identity. Thus, the Marshall Plan, which facilitated Germany's recovery after World War II, in contrast with the humiliating reparations of World War I, led to the development of a healthy, democratic German psyche.

NATO's policy of bombing Yugoslavia is likely to fuel the Serbs' nationalistic pride and determination to overcome another shameful defeat. The critical but perplexing question remains, How can the Serbs become geopolitically strong and secure enough to cut the pathological link between victimhood and national pride and end their need for a "victim-victimizer" psychology?"

Commentary: According to Serbian legend, on June 15, 1389, in the field of blackbirds just before the Battle of Kosovo, in which the overwhelming army of the Ottoman Empire faced off against the Serbian army, a weaker force, an angel appeared before Prince Lazar, the Serbian leader, in the form of a falcon, and asked if he would prefer to die a martyr and ascend to heaven or surrender and live in shame. Prince Lazar chose to die a martyr. After he was killed and his army defeated, the angel appeared beside his corpse, declared him a hero and proclaimed the Serbians as a "chosen people" of God. This battle signaled the defeat of the Byzantine Empire and the beginning of Ottoman Turkish hegemony, which lasted for 500 years.

This legend brilliantly captures the dynamics of the Serbs' humiliating defeat and victimization defensively transformed into a grandiose triumph of heroism and victory. As explained in the piece, the modern-day Serbian genocide against Albanian Muslims who occupied 90% of Kosovo, was clearly in retaliation for the Albanian Muslims' historical genocide against them. This appeared to be motivated by an identification with the historical Albanian aggressors and by displacing and projecting the trauma of the Serbian genocide back into the Albanians, an example of projective identification. Vamik Volkan (1998) wrote about this dynamic relating to the Battle of Kosovo in his book *Bloodline: From Ethnic Pride to Ethnic Terrorism.*

A similar dynamic took place in the Patty Hearst kidnapping, in which she came to identify with her Simbionese Liberation Army (SLA) kidnappers—commonly known as the Stockholm syndrome. Psychologically, it feels preferable to be the victimizer rather than the victim.

The United States resumed its diplomatic relations with Serbia in the early 2000s but, against Serbia's wishes, supported the Albanian Muslims' 2008 Kosovo declaration of independence. The Serbians still consider Kosovo their national heartland, even though it is now almost completely occupied by Albanians. This illustrates the power of an emotional tie that a nation can have to a location, like the Palestinians' tie to Palestine, or the Chinese to Taiwan, or the British to Northern Ireland and Scotland. Psychologically, the historical/cultural tie is extraordinarily difficult to break. However, there now appears to be a break in this Serbian/Albanian cycle of abuse.

Serbia didn't need the patronage of big "parental" powers, like the US, to repair its victim-victimizer mentality and its wounded narcissism. In fact, the US remained an adversary, and in the course of the war, the US bombed Serbian forces in Kosovo. But student opposition and other resistance groups gradually defeated the Milošević-oriented right-wing nationalist party in democratic elections. As a result, the country has experienced a progressive course of privatization and attempts to lubricate and streamline its struggling economic condition, although considerable corruption remains. In addition, it has tried to join the EU and, in this process, has established diplomatic relations with the now-independent Albanian-controlled Kosovo.

A similar victim–victimizer theme is explored in the next piece, which was published in *CounterPunch* on May 22, 2004. This blog discussed the possible motivations of American soldiers in Abu Ghraib prison who tormented and tortured Iraqi Muslim prisoners.

The Underlying Dynamic of Post-9/11 America: Exhibitionistic Revenge at Abu Ghraib

"What is, perhaps, most horrific and incomprehensible about the Abu Ghraib photos are the photos themselves. Why would American prison guards take pictures of themselves smiling triumphantly and making fun of Iraqi prisoners as they humiliated, tortured, and in some instances, raped them? Was this a result of following orders in the dangerous, overcrowded, undisciplined prison milieu of Abu Ghraib, haphazardly trickling down from a chain of command that extended up to Secretary of Defense, Donald Rumsfeld, as Seymour Hersh's *New Yorker* article suggests? Or was it due to some insidious psychological dynamic that not only affected these lower-echelon prison guards, but also the Bush administration's approach to Iraq?

The answer might ultimately lie in the dynamics of exhibitionism: the basic human need to show one's self and be seen. Many psychoanalysts have concluded that the development and preservation of one's fundamental sense of self depends on the need to receive accurate, empathic mirroring. In other words, "I am seen, therefore I am." Humiliating blows to the self-image not only shatters self-esteem and self-confidence, but on the deepest level, can threaten psychic survival. Such narcissistic wounding often unleashes overwhelming rage and the need for revenge, to restore one's pride and self-integrity. Throughout history, this defensive revenge has taken the form of displaying sadistic triumph over a humiliated enemy.

For example, it was commonplace for the ancient Romans to display their defeated scourged, enemies nailed to crosses, for European conquerors during the Middle Ages to parade the heads of their enemies on pikes, and for American Indians and United States cavalry to wear the scalps of their adversaries as cosmetic ornaments. In addition, there have been innumerable wars in which soldiers have murdered their male adversaries and raped their women so that the children born of these unconscionable unions would serve as living exhibits of the conqueror's triumphal image for future generations to come.

Saddam Hussein intimidated his enemies, not only by torturing, raping and murdering them, but by plastering enormous self-aggrandizing pictures of himself on buildings throughout Iraq, as did Mao Tse Tung in China, Joseph Stalin in Russia and Adolf Hitler in Nazi Germany. An awesome publicly exhibited photograph psychologically broadcasts the despot's power, and is intended to intimidate his adversaries and ensure his political survival.

It was therefore not surprising when American soldiers entering Iraqi cities immediately removed Saddam's posters from buildings and encouraged the populace to topple his statutes, to destroy the influence of these exhibitionistic symbols. The ultimate revenge for Saddam's defiance of America was showing photographs of his humiliating capture and videos of him as a defeated, confused, disheveled old man with bad teeth. The videos demonstrated that he had lost his bite.

The same dynamics were evident when Saddam sympathizers in Fallouja mockingly displayed the burned, severed, hanging corpses of American soldiers and construction workers, while dancing triumphantly in the streets. This horrific act of revenge, in addition to instilling terror, was intended to humiliate and destroy America's invincible image and to salvage the shattered pride of Saddam's supporters.

Similarly, the American Abu Ghraib guards were in a frightening, overcrowded prison in which they could have been killed at any moment, within or outside its walls. Although it now appears that some of them may have been operating under orders, their obvious pleasure in photographing themselves triumphantly humiliating these Iraqi prisoners, as if they had nothing to fear, was, clearly, compensatory for their endangered self-esteem and threatened lives. Emasculating and humiliating Iraqi men by posing them hooded and electrically wired, or engaged in homosexual acts, or having them lie on one another nude, or raping them with broom handles and chemical lights, or treating them like animals, wearing dog collars, while laughing and mocking them, gave the impression that these Americans were in total control of a weak, impotent enemy and had nothing to fear. Even if ordered to do this, the psychological drive to take photographs of this sadistic domination must have been so strong that it overrode the obvious judgment that these practices resembled Saddam's and undermined the humanity of America's mission in Iraq.

Subsequently, Al Qaeda exhibitionistically retaliated, displaying a video of the beheading of American contractor, Nicholas Berg, while announcing that it was an act of revenge for the humiliation of Arabs at Abu Ghraib, and intended to redeem Arab dignity. The conspicuous absence of condemnation from most Arab leaders suggested a widespread empathy for this viewpoint. Following Abu Ghraib, a poll indicated that eighty-two percent of Iraqis wanted the United States to end its occupation immediately.

Now we have learned, from Seymour Hersh's investigation, that the photography spree at Abu Ghraib might have been inspired by representatives of a secret undercover contingent of elite operatives, sanctioned by Secretary of Defense Rumsfeld, which had used humiliating photographs of Al Qaeda suspects in Afghanistan and other hot spots to extract vital intelligence data from the suspects' families.

With this possible link to the Bush administration, one wonders to what extent the vengeful exhibitionism at Abu Ghraib might represent, in microcosm, a symptom of America's underlying dynamic after 9/11. After having been profoundly humiliated as the world's greatest superpower by 19 Arab terrorists, the Bush administration has attempted to restore America's wounded pride by humiliating and destroying the Arab world's most powerful despot, Saddam Hussein, and by aggressively and unilaterally imposing democracy on a reluctant, defeated Iraq. How can America establish democracy in the Arab world if its underlying motivation is revenge?"

Commentary: Sadistically exhibiting evidence of a humiliating, ignominious defeat is often used to project power, to intimidate and evoke fear and awe. At Abu Ghraib, this seems to have been partially motivated by the American solders' need to reduce their feelings of helplessness and fear. Since self-image and self-integrity are intimately related to one's basic sense of being, a humiliating image poses a threat to one's existence.

Conversely, a powerful image can be used to influence and intimidate. In *The Wizard of Oz*, the wizard has an intimidating, God-like image, with a frightening voice emanating from behind a curtain. The entire city of Oz is under his thrall, until the curtain is pulled to reveal a small, ordinary man. In many religions, the images of God are portrayed in grandiose, spectacular terms, often accompanied by religious rituals and stories of superhuman feats, for the purpose of convincing parishioners that they can be saved only by submitting to God by praising and worshipping him or her. In this instance, the grandiose image is used to facilitate idealization that unconsciously gratifies needs for safety, caretaking and protection.

This reminds me of my experience of awe as I beheld huge, monumental statues of Ramses II in Karnak, Egypt, and then my shock at seeing his diminutive, fragile mummified corpse under glass in the Cairo museum.

We can see this political dynamic displayed in Trump's exhibitionistic and self-aggrandizing bragging about his superior wealth and business prowess while denigrating and shaming his perceived enemies. Moreover, by portraying himself as a savior who knows how to win, and fix America's problems, he evokes idealization from his base of supporters, especially white male blue-collar workers who have felt ignored and unsupported by the political establishment.

In the next piece, published in the *Huffington Post* on April 28, 2015, on the 100th anniversary of the Armenian Genocide (April 24, 2015), I wrote about president Barack Obama's refusal to honor his campaign promise to acknowledge the legitimacy of the Armenian community's claim that Turkey had committed genocide against Turkish Armenians in 1914. He might have feared losing Turkey's military support for America's wars in Syria, Iraq and Afghanistan, but his failure to fulfill this promise was unjust and made him and America look gutless.

Compromising America's Moral Integrity
Versus Ensuring Military Support

"April 24th was the 100th anniversary of the Ottoman Turkish genocide against Christian Armenians, in which over one and a half million
Armenians were murdered. This has left an unbearably painful traumatic
wound in the psyche of the Armenian community and a devastating blow
to their national self-esteem. They demand that Turkey accept responsibility and guilt for this atrocity. Turkish President Erdoğan contemp-
tuously mocks such pressure from Armenians and others as "misguided,"
calling Pope Francis's statement, "nonsense" that this was "widely considered the first genocide of the 20th century." He defends the slaughter as
a regrettable but justifiable result of civil war. With President Obama and
his advisors refusing to name this atrocity "genocide," as he had promised
Armenians in his 2008 presidential campaign, based on incontrovertible
historical proof, he chose to appease President Erdoğan for fear of losing
his military support in the Middle East. Sadly, Obama joins an inglori-
ous pantheon of Holocaust deniers, including all American presidents
since 1915. This has had the effect of pouring more salt in the Armenian
community's post-traumatic wound. The most poignant analogy would
be the impact on Jews of denying Hitler's genocide against them. Even
Germany an ally of the Ottoman Turks at the time of this massacre, the
European Union, and most American and European newspapers use the
term *genocide* to describe this tragedy.

From a psychoanalytic perspective, naming something identifies its
reality. Refusing to name it implicitly denies its existence. The most salient
psychological issue is whether appeasing Turkish President Erdoğan to
ensure his military backing was worth compromising America's moral

integrity. Appeasing a dictator has a morally repugnant connotation, since Neville Chamberlain's appeasement of Adolf Hitler. The question is whether America can afford to risk losing Turkey as an ally? I believe the answer is yes! America is the most powerful country in the world, militarily. Although Middle Eastern terrorism poses a threat to our country, it is far from endangering our survival at this time. Moreover, we have numerous allies in the region, including Israel, Jordan, Kuwait, the United Arab Emirates, Saudi Arabia and Iraq. The loss of Turkish bases would undoubtedly make it difficult for us, but we would be more than able to adequately compensate in our fight against terrorism. The weakening of America's moral integrity was not worth this appeasement. President Obama, as America's chief representative, appeared hypocritical, not only to the Armenian community and America at large, but also in the eyes of the world.

The vast majority of Americans would have been proud of him and our country if he had the courage to honor his promise and stand up to the political blackmail of a dictator by recognizing and using the term *genocide* instead of further tearing the scab off the intergenerational wound in the Armenian psyche. President Obama still has the opportunity to repair the damage. I would strongly encourage him to revisit this challenge and honor his promise."

Commentary: Clearly, my position in this piece is somewhat cavalier and one-sided, urging President Obama to honor his promise of calling the early-twentieth-century Turkish atrocity against the Armenians *genocide*. Perhaps the threat of losing Turkey's military support, when all military alternatives were considered, was too risky for America.

However, when Hitler invaded Poland in 1939, he told his commanders "to send to death mercilessly and without compassion, men, women and children of Polish derivation and language." He added, "Who, after all, speaks today of the annihilation of the Armenians?" (quoted in *Wall Street Journal*, January 29, 2018, Op-Ed, Robert M. Morgenthau). As a Jew, I viscerally identify with the importance of General Eisenhower's shocking first exposure to victims of the Holocaust in Nazi Germany on April 12, 1944, at Ohrdruf, a subcamp of Buchenwald concentration camp, and his encouragement of British allies to actively find and expose similar atrocities in other parts of Germany.

Unlike Turkey, Germany acknowledged and took full responsibility for its genocide against Jews, Gypsies, gays, the mentally disabled, Catholics, etc., and passed legislation to outlaw anti-Semitic acts and speech. Of course, Turkey wasn't a conquered enemy, and it could freely characterize the Armenian Genocide as a legitimate military strategy since Turkey viewed Christian Armenians as potentially complicit with and aiding its Russian enemies. But regardless of Turkey's stand, other nations like the United States need to acknowledge this atrocity as genocide to help repair this traumatic intergenerational wound in the Armenian psyche. Attorney Robert M. Morgenthau, in an op-ed for the *Wall Street Journal* (January 29, 2018, page A15), hoped that Trump would have the courage to acknowledge the Armenian Genocide because of his bold acknowledgement of Jerusalem as the capital of Israel, unlike Presidents Bill Clinton, George W. Bush and Barack Obama, who reneged on their promise to do so.

Like the Eagleton piece, this was an article of advocacy. Clearly, I didn't know the military risk of losing Turkey's support. But hardly any American news stories at the time were confronting Obama about this issue, and I strongly felt that someone should.

Chapter IX

PRESIDENT TRUMP, "HIS MAJESTY, THE BABY"

1. Trumping Americans: The Strange, Irresistible Appeal of a Narcissistic Bloviator *(Huffington Post, 2015)*

2. Trumping American Democracy: The Frightening Rise of a Fascistic Authoritarian *(International Psychoanalysis, 2015)*

3. America's "White-Lash" and the Degradation of Reason *(Huffington Post, 2017)*

4. Trump's Narcissism: A Key to His Success and Tragic Flaw *(Huffington Post, 2017)*

Lord Acton (April 5, 1887) said, "Power tends to corrupt, and absolute power corrupts absolutely. Great men are often bad men." Although this classic declaration has considerable face validity, it omits the fact that corruption induced by power is often fueled by the psychodynamics of narcissism. Narcissism pervades politics, and politics attracts narcissistic personalities (Wolson, 2011).

The socially inappropriate manifestation of narcissistic traits is what initially shocked so many Americans about Donald Trump's campaign for the Republican presidential nomination in 2015, and continues to do so. Incredibly, lay people and the media, especially liberals and independents, have been effectively transformed into "psychologists" in reaction to Trump's infantile antics and have diagnosed him at best as an egocentric, unreliable person. With palpable alarm, they have severely criticized his glaring narcissistic traits, which many believe make him unsuitable for the presidency.

Without any political education or experience, Trump chose to run for the most powerful political position in the world and won. Declaring that victory would be easy for him, he won the election through egocentric bravado and representing himself as the country's authoritarian savior. Trumpeting his success in business, he claimed that he knew more than the politically seasoned Republican presidential contenders he was competing against. His self-aggrandizing superiority extended to declaring that he knew more about the military than the generals, more about judging than the Supreme Court, etc. Unapologetically, he mocked and belittled his fellow Republican candidates; made bigoted and racist accusations against Mexicans, Muslims and immigrants; devalued women as merely sexual objects; debased Hillary Clinton as a criminal who should be locked up; implied that John McCain was not a hero and was weak for getting captured; made fun of a deaf reporter, etc. He expressed no shame, guilt or remorse for this unconscionable behavior.

From the start of his campaign for the Republican nomination, Trump was boastful and mendacious, and he acted like a child bullying his playmates. Most Americans, journalists and media commentators were astounded and appalled by his scabrous antics but could not take their eyes off him. We all became "looky-loos," who would anticipate with dread and perverse fascination, what new outlandish thing Trump would do or say each day. What surprised me most was the large group of Americans who loved Trump's scurrilous attacks on minorities, the media and the political establishment. Sadly, insidious racism among large swaths of the American public became all too evident.

At the start of his campaign, these issues and Trump's unusual ability to attract attention through the media, without having to pay for advertising, provoked me into writing the following blog, which was published in the *Huffington Post* on August 13, 2015.

Trumping Americans: The Strange, Irresistible Appeal of a Narcissistic Bloviator

"What thoughtful Americans are asking is, why are Donald Trump's outlandish egotistical, self-aggrandizing, racist and misogynistic rants elevating his political ratings to double-digit leads over all other GOP presidential candidates? Why would a narcissistic bloviator, defined in the Urban Dictionary as a "pompous blowhard, using their celebrity to speak about topics on which they are totally unqualified," generate the largest audience for a political debate in the history of this country? On *Meet the Press* last Sunday (August 9, 2015), *New York Times* columnist David Brooks speculated that the answer must lie in the unconscious of America's psyche?

What might these unconscious psychodynamics be?

In the '40s' and '50s but rarely today, vanity was not only regarded as one of the seven deadly sins, but also its overt displays, such as bragging, were judged as shameful and lacking character. Parents raised their children to be appropriately humble about their achievements and good fortune, and to realize that it was impolite to show off. They were taught to resist their infantile wishes to trumpet their superiority and privileges in order not to make their peers feel inferior or less fortunate than themselves. Movie heroes portrayed by John Wayne, Gary Cooper, Gregory Peck and Humphrey Bogart served as paragons of quiet, self-reserved integrity.

In his seminal paper, *Civilization and Its Discontents,* Sigmund Freud theorized that human beings organize into societies that serve the function of repressing (i.e., banishing from consciousness) and controlling their primordial sexual and aggressive impulses, so that they can get along with one another. In the conservative '40s and '50s, the *Leave it to Beaver* generation, the repression barrier was quite strong, and in the late '60s, '70s and '80s, there was a backlash of narcissistic impulsivity, as if the thin veneer of civilization had cracked wide open.

Christopher Lasch called the '70s, a "culture of narcissism." In 1987, Gordon Gecko in the movie *Wall Street* proclaimed that "Greed is good," and in the 2013 movie *The Wolf of Wall Street,* the same narcissistic premise was enacted, highlighting the fact that it was no longer shameful to be a narcissistic bloviator, like Trump.

But what is its appeal?

Some say they like Trump because he is authentic. He doesn't censor himself. He speaks the truth in contrast to politically correct politicians who are so cautious that they seem like hucksters. The psychodynamic in this instance is the pleasure of identifying with someone who doesn't care about social propriety or offending anyone. He does what unconsciously we would all like to do, to express our most primordial aggressive feelings and thoughts without being restricted by guilt, shame or remorse. This is what we did as young children before we were reprimanded for it, and became "socialized." Trump releases us from the straightjacket of being civilized. His unrestricted expulsion of denigrating and devaluing aggression can be confused with truthfulness. In this instance, truthfulness is defined as impulsively saying whatever one thinks regardless of the social consequences. But when Trump says that the Mexican government is sending rapists and criminals across our border, and cites his evidence as the scuttlebutt from some border patrol agents, he is not telling the truth. He is presenting speculative gossip as truthful fact. Or when he says that Iran is financially supporting ISIS apparently without realizing that ISIS is their Sunni enemy whom they are fighting through Shiite militias in Iraq, he is merely vilifying Iran with a calumnious fantasy from his free associations of the moment, like a child who confuses wish fulfillment with reality.

Why have the other GOP presidential candidates and the American public, including journalists, been so silent about his blatantly racist remarks against Mexicans? Does this reflect an underlying prejudice in the American psyche that he has tapped into in which many Americans silently agree with him? Certainly, this has not been the case in his "blood" rant against Megan Kelly, for which candidates in both parties attacked him. And yet many candidates and prominent politicians have remained silent about this as well.

Trump even had the incredible chutzpah to claim that he will get the Mexican and women's vote and that he will represent and help women better than Hillary Clinton. This brings us to another unconscious dynamic in the American psyche, Trump's competitive one-upmanship. He presents himself as bigger and better than anyone else. He frequently says, "I can do anything better than you. I am rich. I am successful. I am the best." The American ethos of rugged individualism and the competitive entrepreneurial spirit pervades the American spirit. Many people have said they like Trump because he is a rich, successful businessman. The more he brags about his success, the more they can live vicariously through his egotistical boasting. To quell his braggadocio would be to deprive them of their dreams.

And last but not least, he is exceptionally entertaining. Since he is a loose cannon, one never knows what he is going to say, how he is going to insult someone, or make some absurd pronouncement and upset the "politically correct" applecart of a serious, formal presidential contest. In a way, he's like the king's jester, the only one who can make fun of the king without losing his head. Only in this instance, the king, metaphorically speaking, is the serious formality of a presidential nominating process and civilization itself, writ large. In contrast to the days of old, however, this jester is actually striving to be king.

The question on everyone's mind is, Will Trump's unconscious appeal to Americans win the day and confirm Alexander Hamilton's warning about democracy: "distrust the wisdom of the masses," or will Americans accurately perceive him wearing "the emperor's new clothes?"

Commentary: The impulse to identify with an anti-establishment, immoral anti-hero is developmentally built into all of us, according to Freud (1914). This is because our primordial narcissistic aggressive and sexual impulses are largely dormant but unconsciously lying in wait and vulnerable to provocation. The allure for us to be "above the law" is a throwback to the time when we were two or three and had not yet become socialized. Thus, part of Trump's popular appeal is motivated by unconsciously identifying with his scabrous, infantile behavior. This psychodynamic is highlighted in "All Our Children: The Inner Appeal Of America's Primal Families" (page 106), when the Clintons, who were leaving the White House and the Sopranos, in their second season, were America's most riveting families. As with Trump, I speculated that this was because of Americans identifying with the Clintons' and Sopranos' impulsive sexual and aggressive boundary crossing: acting above the law.

Trump's inclination to bloviate is another interesting dynamic. When left to his own devices during his campaigning, he frequently didn't make sense. He went off topic, became tangential and said whatever was on his mind. He frequently contradicted himself and changed his opinions. He seemed to react to whatever impulsively struck him in the moment, such as the rumors of border security guards that illegal Mexicans were rapists and criminals. In psychoanalysis, free association is desirable in an analysand in the service of regression and deep analysis. But in an American president, it is potentially catastrophic. President Warren G. Harding (1921–1923) was a notorious bloviator but, compared to Trump, relatively harmless. Nonetheless, Trump's supporters equate his bloviating with authenticity.

During Trump's campaign, many friendly, concerned advisors tried to control his oral effusions and impulsivity by encouraging him to listen to experienced politicians. But these efforts failed. Trump was too grandiose and omnipotent. He knew all there was to know. Tony Schwartz, the ghostwriter for Trump's best seller, *Trump: The Art of the Deal*, reported that he couldn't get Trump to sit still and talk to him. Trump was always in motion. Schwartz had to follow him around and catch whatever he could, on the fly. He believed that Trump could not focus or concentrate on any issue, and that he suffered from ADHD.

Intelligent Americans are wondering if Trump is capable of thinking coherently, deeply and consistently about anything, or learning from experts who know more than he? His past sheds some light on this issue. According to Kranish and Fisher's biography, *Trump Revealed* (2016), Trump was a discipline problem in elementary and high school. This was reportedly why his father sent him to the New York Military Academy to complete his high school education. When he wasn't allowed to defy authority, he responded attentively to instruction and performed well. More on this later (see page 177).

During his campaign for the Republican nomination, Trump's authoritarianism began to escalate. On January 23, 2016, at a rally in Iowa, he claimed, "I could stand in the middle of 5th Avenue and shoot somebody and I wouldn't lose voters." At another rally, he encouraged his audience to violently attack protestors. He also declared that if he were president, congressmen would follow his orders and that if he didn't like what the press said, he would sue them for libel. His nationalistic, "America First" ideology and denigration of other countries and their "exploitative motives" were right out of a narcissist's playbook. "America First" reflected "Trump first." Only he could fix America's problems, not Congress or the courts. There was no recognition of the need for a balance of powers to check an unconstrained president.

His implicit narcissistic ideology was that "it's a dog-eat-dog world" with everyone out to exploit you. For protection, you must fortress yourself against external predators through a strong military and an egocentric nationalistic self-reliance under an authoritarian president. America should be secure in its "splendid isolation," which Kernberg (1975) defined as a symptom of a "pathological grandiose self."

Trump's authoritarianism was applauded by right-wing European nationalists, like politician Nigel Farage, British Brexit advocate, Marine Le Pen, a far-right French presidential contender, and the AFD in Germany. The Ku Klux Klan and the Alt Right newspaper, *Breitbart,* formerly edited by Steve Bannon, praised Trump's racist, anti-immigrant nationalist agenda. I, and many others, began to fear that the American people might elect a fascistic authoritarian Trump as president. This motivated me to write the following blog, which was published in *International Psychoanalysis* on May 17, 2016.

Trumping American Democracy:
The Frightening Rise of a Fascistic Authoritarian

"NOW that Donald Trump has become the presumptive Republican nominee for president, and as violence escalates between his supporters and protestors, with Trump fueling the flames, his self-aggrandizing, insulting and entertaining appeal among thoughtful Americans has given way to the frightening possibility of a fascist demagogue being elected president. Many citizens in both political parties worry that our democracy's checks and balances, freedom of speech, and diversity of public opinion may not be strong enough to prevent this from happening.

Before considering this possibility, we need to determine if Trump is fascistic, and what national psychodynamics are necessary to facilitate its rise, as it did in 1930s' Germany under Adolf Hitler and in Italy under Benito Mussolini. According to dictionary.com, "fascist governments are dominated by a dictator, who usually possesses a magnetic personality, wears a showy uniform, and rallies his followers by mass parades; appeals to strident nationalism and promotes suspicion or hatred of both foreigners and 'impure' people within his own nation, such as the Jews in Germany... Identification of government with a single charismatic leader (the 'cult of personality') is the cornerstone of fascism." Such governments are politically right-wing.

Stunningly, Donald Trump's campaign behavior and political agenda have a remarkable resemblance to these fascistic traits. As a charismatic leader, he has created a "cult of personality" that appeals to a large swath of enraged right-wing Republicans, including white blue-collar workers, evangelicals, Tea Party members, and the Ku Klux Klan (KKK). Instead of "donning" a helmet and showy uniform, he brandishes a wavy blonde combover and sometimes a red trucker's cap. He brags about filling "huge" stadiums with thousands of idolaters who chant his name, reminiscent of Hitler's crowds at Nuremberg. And in the recent past, he has commanded his audiences to raise their hands and pledge their allegiance to vote for him. At a Las Vegas rally on December 15, 2015, a Trump supporter yelled, "Sieg Heil," as a Black Lives Matter protestor was forcibly removed from the audience, and on March 9, 2016, in Fayetteville, North Carolina, a black protestor was sucker punched by a 78-year-old white Trump supporter, as he was being escorted out of the rally by police. Trump is considering paying this man's lawyer fees. At a previous rally, Trump had said he wanted to punch protesters in the face, and that in the old days, protestors would be carried out on stretchers. Moreover, he has threatened, if elected, to restrict media coverage of protests with tougher libel laws, limiting freedom of speech. With omnipotent certainty, he has declared that he will get anyone, including Members of Congress, to do what he tells them, and, of course, get Mexico to pay for the "beautiful" wall he will build on our border to keep illegals out.

With the campaign slogan "Let's Make America Great Again," Trump stokes "strident nationalism," extolling American superiority while devaluing other countries as inferior and as predatorily exploiting America. Like Mussolini and Hitler, he "promotes suspicion and hatred of foreigners," such as Mexicans, Syrian refugees and Muslims, and denigrates women and the disabled.

The psychological seedbed of fascism is extreme frustration and anger, often triggered by an economic depression and a shattering blow to a nation's self-esteem. This results in a pervasive sense of national despondency and helplessness. By idealizing a charismatic, angry national leader and identifying with his perceived power, an economically depressed nation attempts to triumph over its feelings of humiliation and futility. In the process of merging with the idealized leader, people often lose their capacity to think independently. This is what happened to so many Germans who identified with Hitler as their savior.

The fascist leader lifts his people's depressed spirits by disowning and projecting their national sense of weakness and inferiority into minority groups whom he scapegoats for these unacceptable traits. Such scapegoating often takes the form of excluding, attacking and sometimes committing genocide (as Hitler did against Jews, Gypsies, homosexuals and the mentally ill). Through such violent displacement, the fascist leader vicariously evacuates and ethnically cleanses his nation's unbearable self-loathing while cathartically expressing its frustrated rage.

We never thought that American democracy could give rise to fascism, yet so many Americans are being swayed by and voting for what appears to be a fascistic leader. The major cause appears to be the fact that America has barely recovered from the 2008 recession. Although it has fared better than virtually any other country economically, many Americans, especially in the Rust Belt, have lost their jobs to outsourcing and are depressed and enraged over a gridlocked political establishment that has not helped them but enabled the rich to get richer. Moreover, America's pride as the strongest country on earth has been severely wounded by its military failures in Iraq, Afghanistan and Syria, continuous terrorist threats from ISIS and Al Qaeda, and the nuclear specter of North Korea and Iran. This has made our nation ripe for an authoritarian savior, as confirmed by the recent research of Stanley Feldman and Jonathan Weiler. They concluded that economic hardship and terrorist threats from foreigners have increased Americans' "authoritarianism"— the need for a strongman to impose order, security and deal harshly with terrorist threats. This same fascistic pattern is occurring all over Europe in economically challenged countries who are threatened by the influx of Muslim refugees.

This has given rise to white supremacy movements and right-wing demagoguery: Marine Le Pen in France and the AFD (*Alternative für Deutschland*) in Germany. In the catastrophic event that Trump wins the presidency and Congress remains gridlocked, he is likely to rely upon executive orders to achieve his questionable goals. Such presidential hegemony would further incline America toward a fascist-like government. But this is extremely unlikely from the vantage point of American history. The political ascendancy of American demagogues has been exceptionally brief, like that of the populist, dictatorial Louisiana governor Huey Long, anti-Semitic Father Coughlin, and communist "witch hunter" Senator Joseph McCarthy. McCarthy's witch hunting ended abruptly when Joseph Welch (a U.S. Army lawyer) confronted him in a nationally televised Army–McCarthy hearing with the question, "Have you no sense of decency, sir?" Sadly, public shaming has been ineffectual against Trump, who continues to denigrate minorities, accepts no responsibility for encouraging violence among his supporters, and threatens riots if he is not nominated in a contested Republican National Convention.

But as we have seen, more and more Americans are now motivated to block his momentum, as indicated by the increase in protests at his rallies; the Republican establishment's campaign against him; and the Democratic candidates' outcry against his immature, bellicose tactics. Although Trump is likely to be defeated by this growing wave of anti-Trump sentiment, many Democrats and Republicans remain frightened. We are left with uncertainty. We don't know if Americans' independent, rational thinking will prevail over an enraged, primitive mob mentality yearning for salvation from a fascistic "strongman."

Commentary: Since Trump's shocking victory as president, the balance of powers in America's democratic government, the diversity of opinion within and between political parties and the constant media scrutiny, have stymied his authoritarian agenda. The Republicans have been unable to repeal and replace Obamacare three times, their main political objective. If they had succeeded, their victory would have most likely been a pyrrhic one. Virtually no health organizations supported the last bill, and, according to estimates, millions of Americans would have either entirely lost their health care or paid substantially higher costs for it. Many insurers were also against overturning Obamacare.

This was a situation in which Republicans, most of whom hadn't read the bill, were determined to pass it solely on ideological grounds, whether or not it was good for the country. Once again, this reflected the political power of ideological tribal passion over logical, empirical reasoning.

As one might have predicted, America's political use of reason has regressed under the Trump administration. I believe this has been motivated mainly by fear and hatred of "the other" among large segments of the population. A week after I published the following article in the *Huffington Post* on August 9, 2017, there was a frightening outbreak of racial violence in Charlottesville, Virginia.

America's "White-Lash"
And The Degradation Of Reason

"America's political psyche has regressed from a mature state of cooperation between Republican and Democratic Parties under the Clinton administration, to the hateful uncompromising gridlock of today's congressional stalemate on the major issues facing the country, what John McCain recently denigrated as "tribal politics." The egocentric interests of each tribe take precedence over America's greater good. Psychologically, this reflects the primitive defense of splitting, in which each party perceives the other in terms of black and white, good and evil, "My way or the highway." Other symptoms include the degradation of reason, ethics and morality, especially by President Trump and his administration.

What has caused this regression in America's politics?

The reasons are probably multifold, such as frustration with the slow growth of our economy, the fear of terrorist attacks after 9/11 and the wars in Iraq, Afghanistan and Syria, but I believe the main determinant has been an insidious xenophobic reaction to the expanding multicultural complexion of American society. So long as white, Christian, heterosexual, male culture was the American majority, the "otherness" of minorities could be varyingly tolerated. But when blacks, Mexicans, Asians, Muslims, etc., began living in more and more previously all-white hamlets in American society, combined with the traumatic effects of the 9/11 Arab terrorist attacks against our country , a self-protective "white-lash" festered and surged. President Barack Hussein Obama was arguably the last straw, auguring the death knell for white male hegemony.

In my opinion, this existential threat to white America precipitated a regression from mature political intercourse to hateful tribal gridlock. President Trump vicariously expressed the seething nativist longing to make America "white" again. When your tribe is endangered, emotional loyalty triumphs over reason and morality. It's "My family, right or wrong," not "Let's understand each other and work out our differences." Identity politics reigns and "the other" becomes the enemy.

The fear of others is endemic to the human psyche from birth. According to Sigmund Freud, the baby begins life in a state of primary narcissism, in which it experiences everything as part of its self. The first experience of "otherness" is aversive and threatens the baby's psychic survival. This happens when the baby is thrust from the womb's protective refuge and is bombarded by external stimuli. Gradually the baby senses its vital dependency on mother, its first human "other," and through its experience of her protective caretaking, identifies with her and other family members. But strangers then become the threatening "other," until the child comes to know and empathize with them. And this fear and defensive hatred of "the others" has a ripple effect, extending to people of other neighborhoods, religions, races, nations and political persuasions.

When one's survival feels threatened by people with different appearances, languages and mores, one can unconsciously regress to the primordial fear of the "the other" and self-protective rage. President Trump expresses this rage at his rallies, especially with his demand to build a wall and have Mexico pay for it, his Muslim travel ban and his new proposal to cut legal immigration by 50% through giving English-speaking, job ready applicants preferred entry. Although his nationwide approval ratings have dipped to 33%, according to recent polls, each of his white male tribes would vote for him today, not just his 35% working class base. Certainly white male blue-collar Rust Belt workers will vote for him to bring their jobs back and for his stance against outsourcing, his anti-immigration policies and his outsider rage against the political establishment that has forsaken them. But his tribal support also includes, albeit ambivalently, Republican moderate and libertarian conservatives, Christian evangelicals and Catholics. Many conservatives, for example, can't stand his egocentric, reprehensible character and his "bromance" with Putin, but believe that he will fight for lower taxes, deregulation, anticlimate change, smaller government, anti-immigration legislation, as well as appoint socially conservative federal judges and justices, like Neal Gorsuch, to the Supreme Court. Christian evangelicals and Catholics find Trump morally repugnant. Yet they will vote against their religious values in order to advance their Christian conservative agendas.

The late Dr. Leo Rangell, President Emeritus of the International Psychoanalytical Association (IPA), in his book *The Mind of Watergate*, Rangell called this refusal by a president and his supporters to tell right from wrong, a "compromise of integrity," an unscrupulous political strategy in which the end justifies the means.

After Obama's presidency and with the hated specter of Hillary Clinton on the immediate horizon, these white, male tribes voted for a lying, misogynistic, racist, egocentric businessman/salesman who exploitatively molded his political agenda to please them. This reminds me of Chance, the simple, gardener in the movie *Being There*, who so impressed important people, including the president of the United States, as they projected their deepest wishes onto his blank, unresponsive face, that they called him "Chauncey," a more distinguished name. At the movie's end, we see Chance walking on water. Trump's tribal supporters projected their dreams onto him. But unlike Chance, a simple, innocent person, Trump transmogrified himself into an authoritarian savior who promised to give them everything they desired.

In this regressed political climate, will Trump ultimately walk on water, like Chance, or will he sink and drown the hopes of his tribal followers? Surprisingly, Trump's outlandish favoritism toward Russia is beginning to unite the Republicans and Democrats against him, as reflected in their passage of veto-proof sanctions against Russia for interfering with the 2016 presidential election. But regardless of whether Trump succeeds or fails, it is important to realize that his administration is merely a regressive glitch in the long arc of American history. Multiculturalism is destined to represent the majority of Americans in the future. And as diverse Americans increasingly empathize and identify with "the other" and xenophobia fades into obscurity, America's political psyche will regain its capacities for reason, ethics and compromise. The question is, when?"

Commentary: The racial violence in Charlottesville, Virginia, cited above, was perpetrated mainly by the KKK and American neo-Nazis. Following this egregious event, in which one protestor was murdered by a Nazi sympathizer driving his car through a crowd, thousands of Americans marched in cities and towns across the nation, against "hate."

Retrospectively, in the 2016 presidential election, Alexander Hamilton's warning about the dangers of mob mentality in a democracy proved both true and false. Trump won the Electoral College vote handily, but lost the popular vote to Hillary by 2.7 million. The Founding Fathers created the Electoral College to correct for a possible "mob mentality" of the popular vote in a democracy that would favor the most populous states. But, paradoxically, Trump's winning the vote of the majority of electors representing the smaller populations in the "Rust Belt," amounted to a triumph of the "mob mentality" of a minority of the general population.

After his first hundred days as president, Trumps' authoritarian executive orders and political aspirations had been successfully blocked by the judiciary and the legislature, even with a Republican majority in both houses of Congress. He wasn't able to pass one major piece of legislation. The checks and balances of our federal government provided an effective constraint against his authoritarian measures. Federal judges blocked Trump's Muslim immigration ban (which was passed by the federal Supreme Court months later) and his executive order to reduce federal funding for sanctuary cities that protected illegal immigrants. Several cities defiantly declared themselves sanctuary cities and are now suing the Trump administration over its punitive measures. Governor Jerry Brown declared California a sanctuary state in defiance of Trump's and Attorney General Jeff Sessions's anti-immigration stance.

In addition, Republican congressmen in the House of Representatives, fighting among themselves, were unable to repeal and replace Obamacare in their first attempt. In their second try, after easing House voting rules to require a mere majority, they passed a revised bill, which didn't survive a Senate vote. Realizing that they didn't have sufficient votes to justify a third attempt, they withdrew the bill. However, they finally passed a bill nullifying the compulsory mandate to have insurance that was needed to fund Obamacare.

Tens of thousands of Americans have rallied against Trump to preserve women's rights and to combat climate change. Although Trump had the lowest poll numbers after his first hundred days of any previous president, he continued to lie about his outstanding accomplishments, touting himself as performing better than any previous president, clearly a "legend in his own mind."

But in spite of his failures and lies, after 500 days in office, on June 7th, 2018, he remains extremely popular with his base, and his general popularity has risen from 33% to 44%. This is still below all other recent presidents at this time in their administrations. At the outset of his presidency, Trump's political agenda was stymied. His greatest achievement had been appointing conservative judge Neal Gorsuch to the Supreme Court. Disgusted with Republican Senate and House majority leaders, Mitch McConnell and Paul Ryan, for their inability to pass legislation reflecting his political agenda, he briefly cozied up to Democrat leaders Chuck Schumer and Nancy Pelosi to get something done. A small minority of congressmen from both political parties advocated working across the aisle. But this bipartisan atmosphere quickly evaporated, and the Republican Congressional majority, with Trump's support, passed a bill to lower taxes for corporations, giving the 1% of rich Americans a monumental profit, with the justification of incentivizing growth. They claimed that "trickle-down economics" would benefit the middle class and labor through increased wages, an economic theory that has failed to deliver in the past. The Trump administration deregulated restrictions on corporate growth across the board, including abolishing many environmental protections. Trump withdrew from the Iran nuclear deal and imposed severe sanctions on Iran while economically threatening the other signatories, including allies, who continued to honor it. He recognized Jerusalem as the capital of Israel, which previous presidents were loath to do for fear of undermining peace talks with the Palestinians. In addition, the Supreme Court ultimately supported his revised ban against immigrants from certain Muslim countries, and Trump and his National Security Adviser, General John Kelley, have supported Attorney General Sessions's abusive "zero tolerance" immigration policy of criminalizing all immigrants seeking amnesty at the Mexican border, and separating young children from their mothers. After defaming North Korean dictator as "little rocket man," Trump recently (June 9, 2018) met with him in Singapore to facilitate denuclearization of the Korean Peninsula, validating the dictator's political status on the world stage.

Thus, for his base and most conservative Republicans, including Christian evangelicals, the Tea Party, Catholic Church and hate groups such as the Ku Klux Klan and neo-Nazis, Trump's first 500 days in office have been an answered prayer. A number of Republicans have objected to some of his policies, such as inducing tariff wars, pulling out of TPP, threatening to reject NAFTA, his apparent preference for dictators (especially Vladimir Putin) over allies, and his unconscionable separation of mothers and children at the border and placing them in detention camps. Special Counsel Mueller's investigation of his campaign's potential collusion with foreign governments, and of his personal efforts to obstruct justice, continues.

Notwithstanding all the professional speculations about Trump's mental instability, chronic mendacity, questionable judgment, unreliability, impulsiveness and infantile egocentricism, Trump's political agenda has remained remarkably consistent since his campaign, and he has successfully fulfilled many of his campaign promises.

How can we explain Trump's unpredictable success in light of the fact that he has been disturbingly egocentric and politically incorrect every day?

My last piece was published in the *Huffington Post* on July 1, 2017. It is about the positive and negative influence of Trump's narcissistic grandiosity. I first applied the concept of adaptive grandiosity to artistic creativity (Wolson, 1995) and then discussed its important psychological role in politics (Wolson, 2009).

Trump's Narcissism:
A Key to His Success and Tragic Flaw

"Americans are shocked on a daily basis by President Trump's infantile, narcissistic behavior: his hypersensitivity to criticism and impulsive, retaliatory insults, such as against MSNBC journalists "Morning Joe" Scarborough and Mika Brzezinski, and his flagrant lying and grandiose hubris, through which he elevates his ego above respect for the responsibility and integrity of the American presidency. His political inattention, poor judgment and ominous self-reliance have resulted in two congressional committees and a special counsel appointed by the FBI investigating him and his campaign for collusion with the Russian government and obstruction of justice, which pundits are comparing to Nixon's Watergate scandal. Instead of "making America great again," Trump's America is rapidly losing its leadership in international affairs. The drumbeat for impeachment grows louder.

Yet what pundits and the media are overlooking is that Trump's egocentric grandiosity is largely responsible for his incredible success in business and politics. His grandiose belief in his potential for greatness motivated him to stick his neck out fearlessly and convince the most prestigious bankers in the world to lend him huge sums of money to revamp failing New York City skyscrapers and Atlantic City casinos, at a time when hardly anybody else was taking such creative initiative. After significant investment failures and deeply in debt, instead of giving up, his incredible belief in himself motivated him to persist and brand numerous buildings and resorts with his name, making him a billionaire.

Moreover, without any political experience, his enormous self-confidence motivated him to compete in arguably the most difficult political arena in the world and defeat seasoned politicians of both political parties. It energized his ambition, enhanced his charismatic appeal and strengthened his persuasive conviction, which ultimately led to his becoming the most powerful man in the world. Ironically, Trump knows this and prides himself on his narcissism, according to biographers Kranish and Fisher (2016). They quote him as saying that narcissistic people are the most successful, and, in a certain way, he is right.

In virtually any professional, business, scientific, artistic or academic field, the most salient leaders are often charismatic, narcissistic personalities. The reason is that when adaptive grandiosity (i.e., when one's grandiosity is accompanied by sufficient ego strength and reality testing) imbues a person with a feeling of extraordinary specialness and an incredible belief in his or her greatness, this inflated self-esteem often fuels one's ambition to work harder to pursue one's goals and to creatively confront the uncertainties of one's field by thinking and acting divergently. This is because a narcissistic person often relies exclusively on himself or herself, and is not dependent on others and traditional ways of doing things. Thus, Trump rarely listens to authorities or advisors. By being one's own self-ideal, many narcissistic individuals become independent thinkers and create new ways of doing things.

However, because of its fragile nature as a defense against dependency and feelings of inadequacy, adaptive grandiosity can easily regress to maladaptive grandiosity (i.e., an omnipotent belief in one's magical control of external reality, a euphoric feeling that you can do whatever you want regardless of human limitations). During experiences of political power, with its intoxicating adulation and euphoria, the politician's adaptive grandiosity often yields to the temptation of regressing to infantile dynamics and omnipotence, unleashing Pandora's box of greed, in all of its manifestations. This results in believing that ethics, laws and traditional rules don't apply and that you can get away with whatever you want.

For example, President Trump evidently believes that he can ignore the Emoluments Clause of the United States Constitution, and profit from his political position by holding onto his private properties while in office. Moreover, he ignored the traditional ethics of separating the presidency from the FBI by allegedly trying to convince FBI director James Comey to be loyal to him by quashing the investigation into Russian collusion by various campaign advisors and to drop the charges against General Flynn. In his interview with Lester Holt, Trump confessed to firing Comey to block the investigation, admitting to obstruction of justice. With maladaptive grandiosity, the emperor believes he should be appreciated in his "new clothes" and for others to perceive him as he desires. As President Nixon said to David Frost in a 1977 interview, "When the President does it, that means it is not illegal."

Surprisingly, what now appears to be maladaptive: his outrageous infantile grandiosity worked beautifully for him on the campaign trail. Through his unorthodox, simple, impolitic way of expressing himself, he appeared to be fresh and authentic to his supporters, who identified with him. He presented himself as America's savior, a businessman who could fix the problems plaguing the country. As a political outsider, he could express rage for the politically disenfranchised against establishment politicians of both parties. He could insult his fellow candidates, women, Mexicans, Muslims, the disabled, and war heroes; blame immigrants for American terrorism; foster violence at his rallies; speak tangentially, even nonsensically; and blatantly lie. Yet he did this with such grandiose self-conviction that his base believed he was a strong, powerful leader who could bring their jobs back and safeguard the country against terrorism and foreign exploitation.

Since assuming the presidency, Trump's maladaptive grandiosity (i.e., his omnipotence) has been confronted with the limitations of reality: a government with checks and balances and a media that is scrutinizing his every lie, every failed promise, and every ethical and legal breach. His approval ratings have plummeted, yet he refuses to listen to his advisors and fellow Republicans who warn him against "tweetstorms."

For so many Americans, it is like watching a Sophoclean tragedy unfold in which the protagonist is inexorably ruined by a fatal flaw. Can Trump evoke the adaptive narcissism that worked so well for him in the past, or has he finally reached his level of incompetence, according to the Peter principle. Each day we watch this tragedy with disbelief, like "looky-loos" witnessing the fragmentation of our revered American presidency as the specter of impeachment hangs over Trump's head like a Sword of Damocles."

Commentary: As oafish, ignorant and concrete as he appears, Trump possesses the insight to realize that he is a narcissist (Kranish and Fisher, 2016), and believes that his narcissism is responsible for his success, as noted in the piece. When you think about it, what could be more narcissistic than making a fortune branding and selling your own name.

How did Trump become "his majesty, the baby," an infantile narcissist? Unfortunately, the information about his childhood is scanty. My conclusions are consequently speculative.

According to biographers Kranish and Fisher (2016), Donald's mother, Mary Anne MacLeod, came from a poor Scottish background and immigrated to America in 1929 with only $50 in her pocket. She lived with her sister and worked as a domestic. Fred Trump, a successful real estate developer, met her at a dance and, after a brief courtship, married her. He treated her like a princess. Although quiet, reserved, and a dutiful housewife, she was reportedly highly materialistic and ostentatiously displayed her Rolls Royce next to Fred's Cadillac in front of their mansion in Queens, New York. She had a dramatic flair, and she wore her blonde hair in a sweeping, bouffant style, along with ornate expensive jewelry and clothing. There is a remarkable resemblance between Donald's flamboyant hairstyle and hers, especially when you see photos of them side by side. (However, his father dyed his hair a magenta color as he aged and also had a comb over.)

Donald has said that his mother is responsible for his showmanship, and has described her admiringly, as warm, loving and shrewd. He doubted that he would ever find a woman with her sterling qualities. And people who knew the Trumps have said that Mary Anne was the most polished among them.

However, Donald's childhood friends have indicated that, unlike his father, they never saw her emotionally involved with him, and she rarely interacted with them. His father was much more actively engaged when he returned from work, asking about everyone's day, and especially interested in Donald. He encouraged Donald's competitiveness, advising him to be a "king" and a "killer."

Fred Trump was a consummate workaholic a domineering personality, and often absent from his household. Emotionally rigid, conservative and thrifty, he reputedly became the most successful real estate developer in Brooklyn. But he indulged his wife and children. And Donald revered him, calling him "My hero and role model." Donald felt that his father understood him. Thus, upon assuming the presidency, he placed a portrait of his father in the Oval Office but not of his mother, until recently.

Donald was reportedly spoiled and privileged. A childhood friend remembered that he had the first color TV and the best electric train set in the neighborhood, and could do whatever he wanted. Since father was usually at work, there was no one home to provide structure and discipline. A maternally neglected but spoiled child is likely to reject his mother and turn to himself as his only reliable caretaker, a narcissistic defense against needing others. In psychoanalytic jargon, the child becomes his own idealized "breast" and believes that the world should revolve around his ego as the center of the universe. For "his majesty, the baby," rules and regulations should not apply. To be criticized or told what to do is a crushing blow to the child's grandiose but fragile self-esteem. After all, no one tells a king or a god what to do.

Although Donald was a natural leader among his friends, a good athlete and exceptionally competitive, he was also a bully, often beating up weaker and smaller children. He dominated his younger brother, Robert, in their childhood play. Moreover, he lied as it suited him and never admitted that he was wrong. For example, he and his friends were fascinated by a wrestler named Antonino Rocco. Trump claimed that the fighter's name was actually Rocky Antonino. When his friends showed him a newspaper clipping with the name Antonino Rocco, Trump insisted that he was right and the newspaper wrong (Kranish and Fisher, 2016).

This refusal to admit and take responsibility for mistakes was possibly reinforced by Norman Vincent Peale, who wrote the bestseller *The Power of Positive Thinking* and who became Donald's pastor at the Marble Collegiate Church in Manhattan. Biographers Kranish and Fisher (2016) say that Trump's father had taken Donald to hear Peale routinely, and that Donald loved his sermons. He could listen to them over and over again. Peale proclaimed that you could get whatever you wanted in life if you believed that your dreams would come true and ardently pursued them. In this endeavor, you never needed to feel shame or remorse about anything. This might have justified Trump's narcissistic belief that to admit guilt, shame or culpability was weak. It took him years to admit that his "birther" accusation against Obama was inaccurate, and recently he reverted back to his original calumny.

Donald who had been disorderly throughout elementary school was frequently reprimanded by his teachers and sent to the principal's office. At the age of 13, he purchased switchblade knives on a trip to Manhattan after watching actors portraying gang members in the musical *West Side Story*. This was the last straw for his father, who sent him to New York Military Academy for disciplining.

Since Donald was so accustomed to having his own way, you would think he would fail miserably in a structured, unforgiving environment. But surprisingly, he thrived. He knew he couldn't defy the rules without severe penalties. "Those guys were really rough," he said about the Vietnam vet instructors at the Academy (Kranish and Fisher, 2016). He not only was capable of obeying the rules, but he excelled in the competitive atmosphere and became a star cadet, rising to the rank of captain. He was an outstanding athlete in baseball, soccer and football and performed better than virtually anyone else at the academy (Blair, 2000). He was even meticulous about keeping his room tidy, making his bed perfectly and spit-polishing his shoes. Moreover, he was highly respected by teachers and peers alike, who apparently didn't perceive him as an egocentric braggart. However, a mentor considered him the most conniving cadet he had ever met (D'Antonio, 2016). Nonetheless, his generally exemplary performance reflected considerable ego strength and an ability to adapt to rules when he had to.

His father supported Donald by visiting the academy every weekend and attending his sports events. He admired Donald's competitiveness, in contrast with his oldest son, Freddy Trump, Jr., who was sensitive, lacked Donald's killer instinct, and left the real estate business to become an airline pilot. Unfortunately, Freddy Jr. died from complications of alcoholism at the age of 43. Donald said that he was so shaken by his brother's death that he refused to drink alcohol or smoke cigarettes thereafter.

In Donald's mid-teens, his father taught him the real estate business from the ground up. Donald accompanied him collecting rent from building tenants, and Fred advised him to save his pennies because they would eventually become dollars. Moreover, he warned his son that the world was a dangerous jungle in which you had to be a "killer" to succeed. Through the mentoring and guidance of father and military school, Donald learned to work hard and discipline himself. At Fordham University, he did well enough during his first two years to transfer to Wharton Business School, where he cultivated a close relationship with a professor who specialized in real estate. His fellow students looked up to him as more experienced and knowledgeable about real estate than they were, and as relating to this professor like a colleague rather than like a student.

Donald aspired to becoming more successful than his father, and didn't heed the latter's warnings about the riskiness of investing in Manhattan skyscrapers.

I believe that the "adaptiveness" of his grandiosity derived mainly from the grounding in reality that he internalized from his father, Norman Vincent Peale, the New York Military Academy and Roy Cohn. He seems to have internalized his mother's showmanship, charisma and flair. These mentoring influences provided him with the discipline and guidance that enhanced his ego strength, and enabled him to have the patience, persistence and fortitude to achieve his ambitious goals. Without such mentoring, his infantile maladaptive grandiosity would have probably undermined his capacity to achieve anything. He would have merely believed he was a great businessman or politician without any accomplishments to prove it.

Unfortunately, as both businessman and President, two roles in which there was no one to stop him from doing things his way, Trump rarely takes suggestions from advisors or controls his impulsive, aggressive enactments. In hindsight, although the military academy and fatherly mentoring provided the internal structures for success, these external regulators came too late in his development to transform his infantile narcissism into a mature personality that would have been able to learn from others and to empathically relate to them rather than exploitatively use relationships primarily for self-enhancement and ego gratification. Thus, Trump has continued to be an aggressive, impulsive, self-centered bully as President of the United States.

The most critical questions on everyone's mind are: Will he be censored and/or impeached, and will he win a second term in 2020? In an interview with NBC's Lester Holt, Trump bragged that his impeachment would receive the highest TV ratings in history, much higher than Bill Clinton's (Borowitz, 2017). Many anti-Trump Americans are fervently hoping that this dream of his will come true.

Chapter X

CONCLUSION: "BREAKING NEWS OF THE DAY"— THE ENDURING INFLUENCE OF POLITICAL PSYCHODYNAMICS

The psychodynamics in these op-ed pieces and blogs continue to be pertinent as history inevitably repeats itself. This can be seen in the analysis of the breaking political news stories at the time of writing this final chapter in the weeks following November 8, 2017.

Hollywood Producers Harvey Weinstein and Brett Ratner; Comedian Louis C. K.; Directors James Tobach and Bryan Singer; Actors Kevin Spacey, Jeremy Piven and Jeffrey Tambor; Radio Personality Garrison Keilor; Politicians: George H. W. Bush, Judge Roy Moore (Alabama Republican Senatorial Candidate), Democratic Senator Al Franken and Democratic Senator John Conyers; President Donald Trump (once again); and Talk Show Hosts Matt Lauer (also a journalist) and Charlie Rose; Restaurant Owner and Chef Mario Batali; and Olympic Women Gymnasts' Doctor Larry Nassar are all accused of sexual predation.

This is not new to Hollywood or politics, but the Harvey Weinstein exposé triggered an avalanche of sexual harassment allegations, sparking the #MeToo and Time's Up movements. Historically, this has been building steam from the Clarence Thomas–Anita Hill hearing in 1991 to the Bill Clinton–Monica Lewinsky imbroglio in 1998, and more recently, the outing of Bill Cosby in 2014, Roger Ailes in 2016 and Bill O'Reilly in 2017.

The "casting couch," through which powerful producers, directors and actors have taken sexual advantage of aspiring actors and underlings, has been well known since the motion picture industry began. For the most part, sexual harassment has involved powerful men preying upon young actresses, although, as in the case of Kevin Spacey and Bryan Singer, young men are also victimized by older male predators. And a transgendered actress and former assistant accused Jeffrey Tambor of lewd and dominating sexual attention. Although a number of actresses have felt they had no other alternative than to submit to molestaton to retain their jobs or advance their careers, many others, in a state of innocence and/or idolatry, were taken by surprise, molested against their will, and raped. It should be emphasized that the victim's collaboration, for whatever reason, does not justify the unconscionable boundary crossing of empowered predators.

Lord Acton's warning, "Power corrupts!" often induces a psychological regression to omnipotence. This partially explains why powerful people frequently act as if they are above the law, as well as above the moral and ethical standards of society. Thus, Alabama Judge Roy Moore's Republican nomination for the Senate was in jeopardy as a result of accusations by his alleged victims, who claim to have been sexually molested by him as teenage girls when he was a District Attorney in his thirties. At that time, his sexual predation was so conspicuous that he was rumored to have been banned from a local shopping mall. The regression to omnipotence also explains why some senators sexually abused young male and female pages in the 1983 congressional page sex scandal and why Trump, in his recorded conversation with Billy Bush in 2005 on *Access Hollywood*, bragged about seducing women by grabbing their "pussies." He boasted, "When you're a star, you can do anything." More than twenty women have thus far accused him of sexual harassment. Recently New York Senator Kirsten Gillebrand called for his resignation, and 56 congresswomen in the House of Representatives demanded a congressional ethics investigation of the sexual misconduct charges against him.

The regression to omnipotence also explains why JFK felt free to frolic with prostitutes in the White House pool (Hersh, 1997), and why so many distinguished American politicians and presidents had extramarital affairs, including Alexander Hamilton, Thomas Jefferson, Andrew Jackson. Franklin Delano Roosevelt, Dwight D. Eisenhower, Lyndon B. Johnson. Gary Hart and William J. Clinton, etc. Even 93-year-old George H. W. Bush was recently accused of squeezing the buttocks of young women, not just in his current dotage but even while president. Unfortunately, the high correlation between empowered individuals and the sexual harassment of underlings is likely to occur in any workplace, or wherever there are substantial asymmetrical power differences in status.

Most recently, Larry Nassar, the doctor for America's women's Olympic gymnastic team, has been accused by over 265 young women and convicted of sexually abusing them. The blame has fallen on respected Olympic team administrators, university presidents, and others who refused to believe the victims when they reported their abuse. Just as in the "Joe Paterno Syndrome" (see Wolson, page 99), there is an inclination toward tribal regression in the human psyche, which results in trusting and believing "respected" authorities over the complaints of disempowered "children" and women.

In addition to power as a stimulant for regression and omnipotence, developmentally-induced misogyny in the human psyche for both men and women (see Wolson, page 133) contributes to the sexual harassment of young girls, teenagers and older women. Surprisingly, Bill Clinton, Roy Moore and Donald Trump have continued to be supported by the base of their respective political tribes regardless of their unethical and immoral sexual transgressions. It's as if their supporters implicitly condone the right of these empowered men to have their sexual way with women. This is similar to the mythical, primitive father in the primal horde (Freud, 1921). They rationalize and justify such sexual infractions as expectable in high-testosterone, powerful leaders.

Perhaps there is a biological corollary to this, as indicated in other primates. For example, male apes compete physically for the right to dominate and sexually possess female apes, and the latter usually prefer these alpha males. This misogynistic dynamic could have the evolutionary function of protecting and prolonging the species.

Although it is about time that the victims of sexual harassment have empowered themselves against their abusers, the radical escalation of finger-pointing accusations without due process of ethical investigations has begun to resemble a witch-hunt. This is psychologically understandable when any oppressed group finally feels the confidence and freedom to fight for its rights. However, unleashing the suppressed wish for revenge can fuel a lynch mob mentality and unfair retaliation against the accused. The public's guilt for its previous denial and inaction toward sexual abuse has probably exacerbated this mob mentality and arguably stifled protests against unfair scapegoating. Ideally, as victims of sexual abuse are increasingly acknowledged and validated, sexual harassment complaints are likely to become more discriminating along with greater receptivity for the misjudged accused to defend themselves through ethical forums.

26 Killed in a Rural Baptist Church in Sutherland Springs, Texas, the Largest Mass Murder in Texas History; Once Again, Are Guns or Mental Illness to Blame?

It is no surprise that the Texas mass killer, Devin B. Kelley, was mentally disturbed. He had been psychiatrically hospitalized for trying to sneak weapons into Holloman Air Force Base after making threats against military superiors while awaiting a court martial for assaulting his ex-wife and step-son. He escaped from the hospital but was soon caught and convicted of domestic violence in a court martial. Kelley served one year of military imprisonment and was dishonorably discharged. However, the Air Force did not enter his violent history into a national FBI database. Thus, he was able to purchase a high-powered assault rifle and massacre 26 parishioners in a Sutherland, Texas, Baptist church.

President Trump, the NRA and American gun advocates immediately blamed mental illness rather than guns. But often people with no prior mental health record become mass murderers, like Steven Paddock, who murdered 56 country music concert-goers in Las Vegas on October 1, 2017. Blaming the mentally ill is often a manifestation of psychophobia, the pervasive fear of what lurks in the unconscious, a fear that is largely responsible for the public stigma of mental illness (see Wolson, 1972, page 37; Wolson, 2000, page 45). Even if mentally troubled individuals committed more gun homicides than psychologically healthy people—which they don't—such knowledge would be unlikely to result in practical solutions.

This is because psychological treatment cannot reliably prevent people from committing mass murders. For example, James Holmes, the mass killer from Aurora, Colorado (Wolson, 2012), was in psychiatric treatment at the time of his movie theater massacre. Although his psychiatrist was fully aware of his homicidal ideation, she could not legally prevent him from murdering 12 people and injuring 70 others because he had not delineated a specific plan.

Trump has scapegoated the mentally ill for gun massacres rather than blaming the ease of owning semi-automatic weapons, yet he rescinded Obama's executive order prohibiting certain mentally disturbed individuals from access to guns.

The evidence is clear and irrefutable. In countries with the toughest restrictions on gun ownership, like Japan, there are virtually no mass shootings. People are killed through stabbings and other lethal means, but the gun homicide rate is miniscule compared with that of America, whose liberal gun laws facilitate mass murders. In America, the tradition of gun ownership, dates back to the Founding Fathers and the constitutional right to bear arms against an oppressive, dominating government, coupled with the powerful psychological importance of guns for the protection of home and hearth and for the pleasure of hunting as a national sport and cultural tradition, as well as the deeper meaning of guns as a symbol of phallic power. These considerations have effectively blinded a majority of Americans to the human tragedy of mass murders. Even when the victims have been children, women, blacks, church worshippers or concert-goers, the emotional identifications of tribal politics, especially among the NRA, the gun lobby and gun owners have prevailed.

The rationalization that with stricter gun laws, criminals would be able to get guns while leaving unarmed Americans defenseless, strains credibility. If this were the case, countries with the strictest gun laws would have equivalent numbers of gun massacres to America's, which is not true. Arguably, the major reason the "Wild West" is no longer wild is that the rule of law and gun control became securely established. Regrettably, states that have passed legislation allowing the "right to carry" guns are risking an escalation of gun homicides and a tragic regression to vigilante law, as happened in George Zimmerman's killing of Travon Martin.

The Politics of Confession Revisited

The recent disparity between the confession of sexual impropriety by Al Franken and the denials by Donald Trump and Roy Moore renews the debate over the value of political confession. On September 2, 2001, spurred by Christian California Congressman Gary Condit's denial of his affair with the missing Chandra Levy, who was later found murdered, I wrote in an op-ed piece for the *Los Angeles Times* (page 111):

"The political confession is pervasively flawed. It provides ammunition for envious attacks on politicians. It arouses and gratifies the public's voyeuristic, prurient interests... . Yet, to the extent that it motivates the public to evaluate whether the transgressor is truly remorseful for betraying the public trust....it remains one of the best litmus tests for determining the politician's capacity for accepting responsibility and care for his constituents."

Senator Al Franken admitted that model and radio sports commentator Leeann Tweeden's sexual harassment accusations were true. She said he had forcibly kissed her during an acting skit and then photographed himself groping her breasts while she was asleep on a military transport plane. The photograph was displayed in the press. Franken apologized, took full responsibility and welcomed a Senate ethics investigation of his actions. When Tweedan was asked by interviewer Jake Tapper on CNN, if Franken's apology was sufficient or if she would want him disqualified as a Senator, she said that his sincere apology was exactly what she hoped for. But other women accused Franken of groping and kissing them without permission, and he was then pressured by Democratic colleagues to resign, which he did.

In contrast, Donald Trump denied during his campaign and continues to deny that he had forcibly kissed and molested more than twelve accusers, calling them liars and threatening to sue them. He never sued them, although Summer Zervos, a *Celebrity Apprentice* candidate, sued him for defamation of character. She claimed that he kissed her on a few occasions and groped her breasts without her consent. Since then, more than twelve other women have accused him of sexual harassment.

When Trump did not comment on the sexual harassment allegations against Judge Roy Moore, pundits speculated that he was avoiding opening this hornets' nest of accusations against him for sexual misconduct. However, he couldn't stop himself from taking this risk and pounced on Senator Al Franken, a political foe, for his admission of inappropriate sexual behavior. Trump's press Secretary, Sarah Huckabee

Sanders—when confronted by reporters about the difference between charges against Trump and Franken—said that Franken should be held accountable because he admitted sexual impropriety, whereas Trump had not. And Trump supported Roy Moore for the same reason: Moore had denied the accusations. Thus, if you don't accept responsibility and deny accusations, Trump and his press secretary ostensibly presume that you are innocent.

Arguably this is why Trump doesn't admit guilt, remorse or shame about his improprieties. Through projective identification, he might fear the media and others will attack him, as he did Franken, and threaten his reputation and presidency. Press Secretary Sanders advocates this jaundiced perspective. Like Trump, she implied that denial of guilt is morally preferable to accepting responsibility. This unscrupulous attitude privileges political expediency over standing up for what is right. A similar judgment might be leveled against Alabama Governor Kay Ivey, who said she believed the women who accused Roy Moore of sexual harassment, but regardless, declared that she would vote for him anyway because he would support her conservative Republican agenda in Washington, such as appointing Judge Gorsuch to the Supreme Court.

In the Age of Trump, morality has become politically relative. In effect, Governor Ivey will vote for a child molester if he supports judges with conservative moral principles. Regrettably, this immoral, exploitative strategy of tribal politics also holds true for Christian Evangelicals, Catholics and conservative Republicans (see Wolson, page 165) who might find Trump's lying, bigoted, misogynistic character reprehensible, but will vote for him for implementing their political agenda. In other words, the end justifies the means. During the Cold War, America severely criticized the Soviet Union for this Machiavellian perspective, because it implied that "might makes right" rather than "right makes might," which Republican Abraham Lincoln courageously advocated in his argument against slavery at Cooper Union on February 27, 1860. Some historians believe that Lincoln's bold pronouncement at that perilous time helped him win the presidency.

Psychohistorian Robert Jay Lifton, who studied the mentality of Nazi physicians during Hitler's regime, applied his construct of *malignant normality* (Lee, 2017) to their unconscionable behavior; this construct also applies here. He observed that any culture could pressure its citizens to conduct immoral, evil actions. This occurred among Nazi physicians who were initially appalled by the heinous medical experiments they were encouraged to perform, but whose moral values were corrupted by the prevailing "malignant normality" that surrounded them. This principle can be extended to tribal, identity politics in which one is inclined to support one's tribal family, "right or wrong," or justify the support through the anticipation of having one's vested interests fulfilled. Thus, regression to tribal emotionality can overpower reason, morality and even reality testing. In the history of American politics, this has arguably never been as evident as during the Trump administration.

In addition, the psychology of cognitive dissonance (Festinger, 1957), also contributes to our understanding of this phenomenon. When there is irrefutable evidence against our core beliefs, cognitive dissonance theory predicts that rather than be convinced that we are wrong, we would continue to support our beliefs through rationalizations and,, even become more convinced that we are right (see Wolson, page 91).

This is also true for blue-state tribal politics. For example, Democrats who knew that Bill Clinton was a serial philanderer as governor of Arkansas, elected him president anyway and continued to support him after lying about his affair with Monica Lewinsky, even after his impeachment. Regardless of his flagrant indiscretions, most Democrats today believe that Clinton was a great president, and many would vote for him again if it were possible.

But returning to political confession, Is it better for a politician to deny sexual accusations like Donald Trump, even with overwhelming evidence to the contrary, or is it better to confess and act morally and ethically responsible, like Al Franken? Christian California Congressman Gary Condit (Wolson, 2001, page 111), who ran on a platform of moral rectitude, refused to admit his affair with the murdered Chandra Levy, and when indisputable evidence surfaced, his career was ruined. His denial made him look like a hypocrite, which irrevocably tarnished his character and reputation. In the piece about this incident, I stressed the importance of the public's psychological need to trust a politician's moral and ethical judgment.

Until now, it appears that Donald Trump's denials of sexual impropriety have not hurt him politically, even with recently disclosed tapes of Trump's lawyer Michael Cohen and Trump discussing hush money payments to Playboy model Karen McDougal, who allegedly had a one-year affair with Trump after the birth of his child, Baron. But Trump's alleged sexual victims, such as porn star Stormy Daniels, are increasingly taking the initiative to sue him and to have Congress hold him accountable. It remains to be seen if this movement, in addition to Mueller's possible evidence of obstruction of justice, collusion with Russia, and other offenses, will lead to Congressional censorship and/or impeachment, let alone removal from office. Thus, the jury is out as to whether denial or confession is a more effective political strategy.

In many instances, as in the cases of Clinton and Trump, tribal politics has triumphed over the public's abhorrence of immoral sexual transgressions. Nonetheless, Bill Clinton has continued to be tarnished by the moral and ethical stains of his sexual predations, which hurt Hillary in her election bid. Roy Moore's denials contributed to defeating him. Psychologically, as far as character and integrity are concerned, there is no alternative to accepting responsibility and guilt for betraying the public trust.

I believe that even if the current movement to hold Trump accountable is unsuccessful, his character will forever remain forever sullied in the American psyche. I would hope that political parties that support unscrupulous, unethical behavior through an unsavory moral relativism would be more likely to be defeated in the voting booth. Many of us are like deer in the headlights, waiting for America to recover from its current regression to egocentric exploitation and tribal wish fulfillment and regain its ethical judgment, moral dignity and respect for the truth.

Trump's Revenge Against Barack Obama

So many of Trump's policies have seemed designed to destroy Obama's legacy. He launched his political career with the "birther" movement, questioning the legitimacy of Obama's birth certificate and accused him of being born in Kenya as a Muslim. Later he admitted that he was wrong but then scapegoated Hillary Clinton for starting the "birther" movement. In addition, Trump questioned the authenticity of Obama's academic degrees and popular writings; falsely accused Obama of wire-tapping his phones at Trump Tower; fought to repeal and replace Obamacare with Trumpcare; pulled out of the Paris Climate Accords and the Trans-Pacific Partnership; nullified the Iran nuclear deal; threatened to kill Deferred Action for Childhood Arrivals (DACA),—and rescinded an Obama executive order that prevented some mentally disturbed individuals from gun ownership.

He appears to be obsessed with destroying Barack Obama's accomplishments at any cost. For example, on October 13, 2017, he signed an executive order nullifying Obamacare's provision for monetarily supplementing insurance companies' extension of health-care benefits to lower-income Americans. Ironically, this will deprive millions of Trump's blue-collar followers of their health-care coverage.

Thus, Trump is widely perceived as President *Revanche* (Revenge) against Barack Obama. Some attribute this to Obama's skewering him at the 2011 White House Correspondents' Association dinner. Obama said: "No one is happier, no one is prouder to put this birth certificate matter to rest than the Donald. That's because he can finally get back to focusing on the issues that really matter, like: Did we fake the moon landing? What really happened in Roswell? And where are Biggie and Tupac?" In the audience, a red-faced Trump, sat rigidly staring straight ahead. Did this humiliating experience motivate him to become President in order to destroy Obama's legacy?

Trump has denied this. Evidently, he considered the presidency long before this roast. Could his antipathy toward Obama be due to a tradition of racism in his family of origin? Fred Trump, Donald's father, was arrested for "failing to disperse" on Memorial Day 1927, when asked to do so by police who were trying to quell a brawl that was triggered by a 1000-man KKK march through Jamaica, Queens. Six other men were also arrested, but Fred Trump was the only one discharged. Some news articles stated that all seven arrested men were wearing KKK robes, but there is no direct proof that Fred Trump was a member of the Klan, just speculation that he was an interested follower.

Donald has emphatically denied that his father was the arrested "Fred Trump." He claims that his father never lived at the address recorded in the police ledger, but investigators have determined that Trump's father was actually living there at the time of his incarceration.

In 1973, Fred Trump's real estate company was successfully sued and fined for racial discrimination against blacks in rental housing. Although in court, the Trumps (Donald had begun to manage the company) promised never to discriminate in the future, they were again sued and fined for discouraging blacks from moving into their rental properties. In fact, folk singer Woody Guthrie, who lived in a Fred Trump Beach Haven rental, wrote the following lyrics: "I suppose Old Man Trump knows how much racial hate he stirred up in the blood-pot of human hearts when he drawed that color line here at his Eighteen hundred family project... Beach Haven looks like heaven where no black ones come to roam! No, no, no! Old Man Trump! Old Beach Haven ain't my home!" (Woody Guthrie, early 1950s).

Racial prejudice in Trump's upbringing is not surprising considering the bigotry he has expressed against blacks, Latinos and Muslims in his campaign and during his presidency. It is not farfetched to speculate that Obama's black presidency galled him tremendously, as it did so many white, working class males who ultimately became Trump's strongest supporters. Sadly, Trump's hatred of the non-white "other" probably helped him win the election.

Perhaps what is most dangerous about Trump's narcissistic revenge against Obama were his withdrawal of America from the Iran nuclear deal and his saber-rattling against North Korea, threatening to launch a nuclear war of "fire and fury like the world has never seen," if Kim Jong Un achieves the capacity to reach the United States with a nuclear intercontinental ballistic missile. However, in his Pacific Asian tour, Trump toned down his warmongering rhetoric and communicated a wish to negotiate. But Kim Jong Un on January 1, 2018, said "the button for nuclear weapons is on my table" and that he could launch a nuclear attack on anywhere in the United States. President Trump took the bait and tweeted on January 2, "Will someone from his depleted and food starved regime please inform him that I too have a Nuclear Button but that it is a much bigger and more powerful one than his, and my Button works." In other words, Trump's phallic power was bigger and more potent than "little rocket man's." Although this infantile pissing contest, with two narcissistically vulnerable world leaders, could have escalated into a nuclear holocaust, fortunately it didn't.

In fact, beginning with peace overtures during the Olympic games in Korea, North and South Korea began angling toward the end of the North Korea–South Korea conflict and working toward peace, and Trump recently met with Kim Jong Un in Singapore, the first American President to meet with a North Korean leader. They both signed a document expressing the intention to denuclearize the Korean Peninsula. Trump's aggressive confrontation of Kim Jong Un might have contributed to these peace overtures. Since this meeting, Trump has spoken about Kim with deep respect and admiration. Moreover, in a surprising peace overture, he unilaterally suspended the annual military exercises between the United States and South Korea to prepare for any possible military engagement with North Korea, to the dismay of South Korea, Secretary of Defense General Mattis and other American military leaders. Many pundits and political analysts have criticized him for yielding political leverage and weakening South Korea's defensive preparation, so that Trump could brag about being a fabulous peace maker. Trump declared that North Korea was no longer a nuclear threat, and intimated that he might even win the Nobel Peace Prize for his efforts.

Unfortunately, the prospect of nuclear war with North Korea remains as grave as ever. No specific program for denuclearization has emerged yet from Trump's meeting, and there are recent (June 28, 2018) speculations that Kim is continuing to expand his nuclear arsenal. Because there are no governmental restrictions on Trump's presidential capacity to start a nuclear war, the prospect of a Trumpian doomsday due to his impulsivity and poor judgment remains an ever-present reality. There is currently a movement in Congress to require American presidents to obtain congressional approval before they launch a nuclear war. However, it remains extremely doubtful that this will become law in the near future.

Political Consequences of Trump's Narcissism

Arguably, Donald Trump's grandiose, narcissistic psychodynamics (see page 172) make him feel that he can say anything publicly and not be held accountable. For example, during campaign speeches he explicitly urged the Russians to hack Hillary Clinton's emails. And now Special Prosecutor Mueller appears to be trying to determine whether Trump supported members of his administration, like his son, Donald Jr., and George Papadopolous, to obtain "dirt" on Hillary through the Russians. It's as if the emperor doesn't expect others to see his "new clothes" (even when he garishly flaunts them), let alone closely examine them and judge him harshly (see Wolson, page 154).

Trump's palpable admiration for dictators like Russia's Vladimir Putin, China's Xi Jinping, the Philippines' Rodrigo Duterte and most recently (June 15, 2018) North Korea's Kim Jong Un is consistent with his not-so-hidden desire to be King of the United States, in keeping with his father's directive. On February 6, 2018, he wanted a military parade down Pennsylvania Avenue in his honor, emulating the display of military might of other dictators. He publicly bemoans the fact that he cannot control the Justice Department or the FBI. And he baldly commented how much he admires Kim Jong Un for having absolute control over his people, and that when he speaks, his people sit up at attention. "I would like my people to do the same," he said. His blatant wish for omnipotent control reveals an unconscionable lack of respect for the separation of powers, the checks and balances of government and a free press (which he has recently attacked as a greater enemy than Russia, China or North Korea), which constitute the core structures of American democracy (see Wolson, page 160). Trump seems to lack any discernable totalitarian ideology. What made Hitler so destructive was that he had a somewhat coherent Aryan belief system that enabled him to mesmerize and dominate the German people. Trump's belief system seems restricted to protecting and aggrandizing his fragile ego. Though this personal Achilles' heel might save America from a Trumpian dictatorship (see Wolson, 2017, page 172), it suggests that his leadership will remain erratic, impulsive and misguided and that America has an extremely bumpy, pot-holed, and potentially dangerous road ahead.

Arguably, the most flagrant manifestation of Trump's authoritarianism appeared in news reports (November 14, 2017) of a draconian White House prohibition of the Centers for Disease Control and Prevention (CDC) and other departments under Health and Human Services (HHS) from using seven words in its budget requests. These words were: *vulnerable, diversity, evidence-based, science-based, fetus, entitlement* and *transgender*. White House advisors allegedly suggested that the word *science* could be used only in with community approval. This astoundingly implied that scientific discoveries would have no independent validity. Social opinion (i.e,, White House political biases) would be the ultimate determinant of scientific reality. If implemented, this would be an anti-scientific regression in which a mob mentality (whether religious, as before the Age of Enlightenment, or political, as in the Age of Trump), would judge what was factual or not.

Of course, this is a manifestation of Trump's narcissistic *modus operandi*. He considers himself the ultimate arbiter of what is real and what is fake news depending on what supports and protects him politically or undermines his agenda. Fortunately, the Director of the CDC (November 17, 2017) indicated a few days later that there was no factual basis to these news reports, and that the CDC was free to employ whatever words it chooses. The directors of other departments who received similar prohibitions did not respond. Some pundits have speculated that the motivation for this Trumpian "thought control" was to implement a right-wing agenda that questioned scientific evidence, diversity, and the rights of the transgendered and abortion advocates. Trump's unwillingness to investigate Russia's meddling in the 2016 election, which might cast doubt on the legitimacy of his presidency, amounts to an authoritarian cover-up.

His narcissistic fears of dependency have influenced his "America First" policy of extricating the US from multinational agreements, such as the Paris Climate Accords, the Trans-Pacific Partnership, and international trade agreements. This has weakened America's historical role as world leader. Trump believes that dependency on other countries makes America vulnerable to foreign exploitation. This is arguably an expression of his narcissistic fears of dependency and a projection of his own exploitative aims. In contrast, he favors negotiating unilateral trade deals in order to have more bargaining power. Unfortunately, his aversion to dependency on other nations has begun to hurt American businesses whose financial success has relied upon multinational agreements.

The *Wall Street Journal* has indicated that few nations are likely to enter into unilateral agreements with the US. For example, during an international tour, Trump wanted Japan to accept a unilateral agreement with America, but Prime Minister Shinzo Abe tried to convince Trump to rejoin the Trans-Pacific Partnership instead. Unfortunately, Trump's "America First" exit from the Trans-Pacific Partnership has paved the way for China to become the most powerful country in the Asian Pacific, and has consigned the United States to a weak, second-class status in this region of the world. The narcissism of "America First" ultimately results in what Kernberg (1975) called "splendid isolation." Unfortunately, this would be far from "splendid" for America.

Ironically, Trump has chosen to depend upon Russian President Vladimir Putin, who is widely known as an exploitative manipulator. Why would Trump make himself so vulnerable? One explanation is that a grandiose narcissist relates best to the "other" by projecting his own ideal self onto him or her (Kernberg, 1975). Thus, Putin would be a reflection of Trump's own ideal grandiose self, and therefore would not threaten him. In effect, Trump would be merely depending upon himself in the guise of Putin. This narcissistic identification explains Trump's curious preference for ruthless dictators over America's traditional allies.

Interestingly, Joseph Stalin might have suffered from this same narcissistic dynamic with Adolf Hitler during WWII, with whom he signed the ten-year German–Soviet Nonaggression Pact on August 23, 1939. In June 1941, when messengers informed Stalin that Hitler was invading and bombing Russia, Stalin was stunned and couldn't believe that his malevolent, dictatorial alter ego would betray him (Montefiore, 2003).

Another possible reason for Trump's support of Putin would be his goal of becoming the first president to make peace with America's most dangerous enemy. In his presidential campaign, Trump announced that this was a presidential goal. And a third reason might be his anti-authoritarianism. As a narcissistic iconoclast, he probably derives pleasure from defying traditional moral, ethical and political expectations. Perhaps this is why he shocks Americans on a daily basis. A fourth possibility is his expectation of benefiting financially from Russian business deals. And the last and arguably most frightening speculation is that Putin is blackmailing Trump with hotel videos of him cavorting with Russian prostitutes or has some other compromising material on him. If true, this would give Putin monumental political leverage over American democracy.

The public's greatest fear continues to be that Trump's egotistical vulnerability, impulsivity, phallic competitiveness and delusions of omnipotence might propel America into a nuclear war with North Korea and/or Iran. In the 2017 book, *The Dangerous Case of Donald Trump*, featuring articles by 27 psychiatrists and other mental health professionals, Trump was assessed as mentally unfit to be president and as presenting a clear and present danger to the security of the United States. These psychiatrists and psychologists felt that their duty to warn Americans of Trump's dangerous psychological condition took precedence over the Goldwater rule, prohibiting the diagnosis of a public figure from afar and without his or her consent.

I heartily agree with their decision and would go further in stating that mental health professionals should contribute to the public dialogue concerning the "breaking news of the day" on an ongoing basis. In my opinion, the public can benefit greatly from a deeper psychological understanding of political events.

Trump's ability to deliver his State of the Union message on January 30, 2018, in a clear and comprehensible presidential manner belies the conclusions of those who have thought he suffers from an inability to concentrate, to focus or to articulate a coherent political agenda. In his speech, he delineated a consistent Republican, conservative program of lower taxes, deregulation, limited government, a strong military, anti-climate change, anti-Obamacare, social conservatism and anti-immigration that he had proposed in his presidential campaign and has tried to implement throughout his first year in office. While he has been unreliable and impulsive, and even appears "loony" at times, he has also consistently been able to follow a political agenda that appeals to virtually 45% of the country. In fact, he now has so much political power that Republicans have become fearful of challenging him, and have been characterized in the media as a Trump cult. As of June 28th, 2018, he is supported by 90% of Republicans, He has effectively transformed their political agenda into the party of Trump—befriending our traditional enemies; starting trade wars with Canada, China and the EU; separating children from their amnesty-seeking mothers; and institutionalizing a standard of scurrilous infantile political discourse.

Ultimately, Trump might be censored or impeached for obstruction of justice or collusion with Russians or defying the emoluments clause in the Constitution, but it is highly unlikely that he will be compelled to resign due to mental instability. A number of American presidents have exhibited flagrant psychological problems, such as Richard Nixon's paranoia, Lyndon Johnson's manic depression/bipolar disorder (Hershman, 2002) (Johnson literally believed that God was selecting his bombing targets in Vietnam), Abraham Lincoln's clinical depression, Ulysses S. Grant's alcoholism, etc., but none were forced out of office due to psychiatric disability.

Conclusion

Fareed Zakaria, on his TV show, *Global Public Square* on Sunday, December 3rd, 2017, declared that psychology and behavioral economists have been exerting a great influence over the understanding of cultural nationalism in America under Trump and in the right-wing movements in France, Germany and Britain's "Brexit." Zakaria said that psychologists have illuminated the ethno-cultural motivations in tribal/identity politics rather than financial economic concerns as the primary cause of nationalism. In support of his opinion, a recent article in the *New York Review of Books* (Ash, 2017) attributed the rise of the nationalistic right-wing AFD in Germany to a fear of the loss of German cultural integrity due to the influx of Muslim Turkish and Syrian populations. The authors believed that this nationalism was not due to deep-seated economic worries, because Germany was doing quite well economically, but more attributable to losing the German way of life to a threatening, foreign "other." A family friend from Brussels expressed similar apprehension, fearing that Syrian Muslims were trying to impose Sharia law in her community and were threatening her Belgian way of life.

A psychoanalytic perspective concerning the unconscious meaning of tribal politics adds depth to this discussion. It is valuable for the public to understand how self- development is intrinsically linked to identification with one's parents and family and how "the other" remains aversive and threatening throughout life until, through empathy and identification, the feared and hated "other" becomes embraced and loved as part of one's self. If empathy and identification are never achieved, "the other" continues to be perceived as aversive and menacing, sometimes for centuries.

The "backlash" of multicultural diversity against the "white-lash" of President Trump and his right-wing supporters symbolizes the hope of America returning to the ideal of what it has traditionally symbolized: a universal, ecumenical country with its Statue of Liberty welcoming the world's persecuted "huddled masses longing to be free." The leading edge of this "backlash" has arguably become the women's #MeToo and Time's Up" movement against sexual harassment and racism. This was poignantly illustrated recently by the 98% of Alabama black women who voted against accused pederast, Roy Moore, and defeated him.

The fight against sexual harassment has profoundly affected both Democratic and Republican Congressmen, who appear motivated to pass legislation that punishes offenders. The bipartisan nature of the women's movement might become what has been politically needed to break through the tribal polarization and political deadlock that has paralyzed Congress for decades from moving forward with interparty compromises and solutions. Since both Republican and Democratic politicians have been found guilty of sexual predation, the women's fight for equal rights could conceivably be a major catalyst to induce our political parties to unite in fighting all forms of bigotry, such as racism, religious persecution, xenophobia and attacks against the LGBTQ community. Some fear that Trump's authoritarian "white-lash" is the road to a future American apocalypse. But I believe it is merely the last-ditch stand of white, male hegemony against the inevitable, inexorable multicultural triumph of "the other" that will ultimately come to symbolize all of us in America.

Similarly, Pope Francis declared in his 2017 Xmas Mass, that the story of Christ's birth is that of an immigrant Jewish minority family in a strange persecutory land, struggling to survive. He focused on the importance of accepting and loving the stranger, the persecuted immigrant "other." In Myanmar, Pope Francis condemned the horrific plight of the persecuted Rohingya Muslim minority by the overwhelming majority of Buddhists.

The basic challenge of the human psyche is to overcome the hatred of "the other," induced by the narcissism of minor and major differences and projective identification, and to realize that each of us—black, brown, yellow, red or white; rich or poor; gay or straight; man or woman—is a member of the same human family deserving of respect and love.

To paraphrase writer-philosopher George Santayana, "Those who cannot learn from history are doomed to repeat it." Unfortunately, political history tends to repeat itself regardless of how much humanity has learned. This is because the underlying psychodynamics that motivate political events are just as likely to recur as they do within the human psyche, through the inevitability of repetition compulsion.

My op-ed pieces and online blogs include a variety of psychodynamic lenses to understand the complex unconscious motivations of political and cultural events. Although numerous, these are merely some constructs from the vast array of psychoanalytic knowledge that could be potentially applied. The constructs I have used include psychophobia, the narcissism of minor differences, the superego in the service of the id, identification with the aggressor, regression, projective identification, exhibitionistic revenge, pride of victimhood, the unconscious allure of being above the law, narcissistic grandiosity and inferiority, narcissistic expediency, ominous self-reliance, splendid isolation, healthy narcissism, adaptive grandiosity, healthy exhibitionism, the developmental hatred of "the other," endemic misogyny, dis-identification, omnipotent control, existential precariousness, healthy and unhealthy idealization, the need for authoritarianism, separation–individuation, sibling rivalry, cognitive dissonance, Oedipal victory and defeat, healthy and unhealthy dependency, superego surveillance, pre-Oedipal and Oedipal psychopathology, phallic initiative and competitiveness, apocalyptic psychology, dependency vs. autonomy, paternal and maternal representations, loss of impulse control, adolescent rebellion, the intergenerational transmission of trauma, the denial of psychological causation, ambivalence, splitting, etc.

In this Age of Trump, when virtually everyone has become an "armchair psychologist," there has arguably been no more important time in modern history for psychoanalysts and psychoanalytically oriented professionals to deepen the public understanding of the cataclysmic political problems that face us. There has been a long tradition of psychoanalytic political writing, but in America, this has been mainly confined to professional journals and books. Joining the media dialogue about the "breaking news of the day" could enrich and enhance American public's understanding of unconscious political motivation while making psychoanalysis more accessible and user-friendly in addition to reducing psychophobia. Ultimately, it might even help resolve the diverse and enduring political conflicts that have plagued humanity throughout the ages.

REFERENCES

Acton, J. (1887). Letter to Bishop Mandell Creighton. In *Historical. Essays and Studies*. J.N. Figgs & R.V. Laurence, eds. London: Macmillan (1907).

Ash, T. (2017, December 7). It's the Kultur, Stupid. In *New York Review of Books*.

Benedict, R. (1934). *Patterns of Culture*. New York: Houghton Mifflin Harcourt.

Benedict, R. (1946). *The Chrysanthemum and the Sword: Patterns of Japanese Culture*. Boston: Houghton Mifflin.

Blair, G. (2000). *The Trumps: Three Generations of Builders and a President*. New York: Simon & Schuster.

Bollas, C. (2018). *Meaning and* Melancholia: *Life in the Age of Bewilderment*. New York: Routledge.

Borowitz, A. (2017, May 12). Trump Boasts That His Impeachment Will Get Higher TV Ratings Than All Other Impeachments. *The New Yorker*.

Cash, W. (1941). *The Mind of the South*. New York: A.A. Knopf.

D'Antonio, M (2016). *The Truth About Trump*. New York: St. Martin's Press.

Erikson, E. (1950). *Childhood and Society*. New York: Norton.

Erikson, E. *Young Man Luther: A Study in Psychoanalysis and History*. New York: Norton, 1958.

Erikson, E. *Gandhi's Truth: The Origins of Militant Nonviolence*. New York: Norton, 1969.

Festinger, L. (1957). *A Theory of Cognitive Dissonance*. Stanford: Stanford University Press.

Freud, S. (1910). Leonardo da Vinci and a Memory of His Childhood. *Standard Edition*. 11:63–137. London: Hogarth Press.

Freud, S. (1913). Totem and Taboo. *Standard Edition* 13.

Freud, S. (1918). The Taboo of Virginity. *Standard Edition* 11:193.

Freud, S. (1920). Beyond the Pleasure Principle, *Standard Edition* 18.

Freud, S. (1921). Group Psychology and the Analysis of the Ego. *Standard Edition* 18.

Freud, S. (1930). Civilization and Its Discontents. *Standard Edition*. 21:64.

Freud, S. (1939). Moses and Monotheism. *Standard Edition*. 23:7.

Hersh, S. (1997). *The Dark Side of Camelot.* Boston: Little, Brown and Co..

Kardiner, A. & Linton, R. (1939). *The Individual and His Society.* New York: Columbia University Press.

Kernberg, O. (1975). *Borderline Conditions and Pathological Narcissism.* New York: Aronson.

Kranish, M. & Fisher, M. (2016). *Trump Revealed: An American Journey of Ambition, Ego, Money and Power.* New York: Scribner.

Lakoff, G. (1996). *Moral Politics.* Chicago: University of Chicago Press.

Lasswell, H. (1930). *Psychopathology and Politics.* Chicago: University of Chicago Press.

Lear, J. (1995, December 25). The Shrink Is In. *The New Republic.*

Lear, J. (1998, March 28). Freudian Slip. *The New Republic.*

Lee, B. (2017). *The Dangerous Case of Donald Trump.* New York: St. Martin's Press.

Mead, M. (1928). *Coming of Age in Samoa: A Psychological Study of Primitive Youth for Western Civilization.* New York: William Morrow.

Minutaglio, B. (1999). *First Son: George W. Bush and the Bush Family Dynasty.* New York: Three Rivers Press.

Montefiore, S. (2003). *Stalin: The Court of the Red Tzar.* New York: Vintage Books.

Rangell, L. (1980). *The Mind of Watergate.* Toronto: George J. McLoed.

Roheim, G. (1934). *Origins and Functions of Culture.* New York: Anchor.

Singer, M. (1961). A Survey of Culture and Personality Theory and Research. In *Studying Personality Cross-Culturally,* Bert Kaplan, ed. New York: Elmsford.

Volkan, V., Itzkowitz, N., & Dod, A. (1997). *Richard Nixon: A Psychobiography.* New York: Columbia University Press.

Volkan, V. (1998). *Bloodline: From Ethnic Pride to Ethnic Terrorism.* Boulder: Westview Press.

Zaretsky, E. (2015). *Political Freud.* New York: Columbia University Press.

Zelnick, B. (1999). *Gore: A Political Life.* Washington, DC: Regnery.

PETER WOLSON'S PUBLICATIONS

OP-ED PIECES AND BLOGS

Wolson, P. (August 20, 1972). Eagleton and America's Psychophobia. *Los Angeles Times* OPINION Section, M.

Wolson, P. (January 24, 1999). Hating the Politician in the Mirror, *Los Angeles Times* OPINION Section, M.

Wolson, P. (May 9, 1999). Politics of Victimhood: A Perpetual Cycle of Abuse. *Los Angeles Times* OPINION Section, M.

Wolson, P. (August 22, 1999). Strange to Say, but Neurotics Are Preferable. *Los Angeles Times* OPINION Section, M.

Wolson, P. (December 5, 1999). When Politics Is Also Psychology. *Los Angeles Times* OPINION Section, M.

Wolson, P. (May 28, 2000). A World of Psychophobia. *Los Angeles Times* OPINION Section, M.

Wolson, P. (November 26, 2000). America's State of Mind: Healthy and Divided. *Los Angeles Times* OPINION Section, M.

Wolson, P. (March 18, 2001). All Our Children: The Inner Appeal of America's Primal Families. *Los Angeles Times* OPINION Section, M.

Wolson, P. (September 2, 2001). The Politics of Confession. *Los Angeles Times* OPINION Section, M.

Wolson, P. (February 14/15, 2004). The Politics of Narcissism: America's Grandiose Persona Under Bush. Weekend Edition of *CounterPunch*.

Wolson, P. (March 11, 2004). *The "Passion" of Anti-Semitism* (unpublished).

Wolson, P. (May 22/23, 2004). The Underlying Dynamic of Post-9/11 America: Exhibitionistic Revenge at Abu Ghraib. Weekend Edition of *CounterPunch*.

Wolson, P. (October 16, 2008). America's Racism: Hatred of "The Other" in the 2008 Presidential Election. *Huffington Post*.

Wolson, P. (October 20, 2008). The Hatred Between Republicans and Democrats: The Conflict Within America's Psyche, Redux. *Huffington Post.*

Wolson, P. (October 16, 2011). Is Stuttering Biological or Psychological? *Huffington Post.*

Wolson, P. (November 10, 2011). The Joe Paterno Syndrome: Idealization and the Corruption of Morality. *Huffington Post.*

Wolson, P. (July 3, 2012). The Aurora Massacre: Coping With the Precariousness of Human Existence. *Huffington Post.*

Wolson, P. (October 1, 2012). Does Dependency on Government Make Americans Weak? A Psychoanalyst's Perspective. *Huffington Post.*

Wolson, P. (December 20, 2012). The Fiscal Cliff: D.C.'s Mayan Apocalypse. *Thomson Reuters.*

Wolson, P. (April 28, 2015). Compromising America's Moral Integrity Versus Ensuring Military Support. *Huffington Post.*

Wolson, P. (May 21, 2015). The Bush Boys: No Sibling Rivalry, but Maybe Something Deeper. *Thomson Reuters.*

Wolson, P. (August 13, 2015). Trumping Americans: The Strange, Irresistible Appeal of a Narcissistic Bloviator. *Huffington Post.*

Wolson, P. (May 16, 2016). Trumping American Democracy: The Frightening Rise of a Fascistic Authoritarian. International Psychoanalysis.com

Wolson, P. (May 27, 2016). The Puzzling Vilification of Hillary, A Psychoanalyst's Perspective. *Huffington Post.*

Wolson, P. (July 1, 2017). Trump's Narcissism: A Key to his Success and Tragic Flaw. *Huffington Post.*

Wolson, P. (August 9, 2017). America's "White-Lash" and the Degradation of Reason. *Huffington Post.*

PROFESSIONAL JOURNAL AND BOOK ARTICLES

Wolson, P. (1995). The Vital Role of Adaptive Grandiosity in Artistic Creativity. *The Psychoanalytic Review.* 82:577–597.

Wolson, P. (1995). Some Reflections on Adaptive Grandiosity in Fatherhood. In *Becoming a Father.* J. Shapiro, M. Diamond, & M. Greenberg. New York: Springer, Chap. 24.

Wolson, P. (2005). The Existential Dimension of Psychoanalysis (EDP): Psychic Survival and the Fear of Psychic Death (Nonbeing). *The Psychoanalytic Review.* 92:675–699.

Wolson, P. (2009). Political Power: An Alluring stimulant for Regression and Omnipotence. In *Greed: Sex, Money, Power and Politics.* R. Ronis and L. Shaw, eds. New York: International Psychoanalytic Books. (2011), pp. 141–154.

Wolson, P. (2011). The Seminal Therapeutic Influence of Analytic Love: A Pluralistic Perspective. Eds. M. Diamond, and C. Christian. London: Karnac, Chap. 8.

Wolson, P. (2012). Working with the Relational Unconscious: An Integration of Intrapsychic and Relational Psychoanalysis. *The Psychoanalytic Review.* 99:209–225.

Wolson, P. (2018). Political Freud by Eli Zaretsky (book review). *Psychoanalytic Psychology* (issue to be announced).

Index

abortion, 83

Abu Ghraib torture and prisoner abuse, 142–46

abuse

  a perpetual cycle of, 138–42

  See also Abu Ghraib torture and prisoner abuse; sexual transgressions

Acton, Lord (John Dalberg-Acton, 1st Baron Acton), 115, 151, 182

adolescent rebellion, 59, 61, 65, 66, 82, 135

Adorno, Theodore, 16, 17

Affordable Care Act. *See* Obamacare

African Americans. *See* Obama, Barack; racism; white-lash; white supremacy

ambivalence, 26, 74

anonymity, analytic, 20–21

anthropology, cultural, 14–16

anti-Semitism, 74–80

  as an expression of repressed hatred toward Christ, 78

  envy of Jews and, 78–80

  The Passion of the Christ and, 74–78

  Passion Plays and, 74, 77

  projective identification and, 74, 77, 80, 124

anxiety. See existential anxiety

apocalyptic psychology, 90–94

Armenian Genocide, 147–50

Aryan race and superiority, 125, 134, 139, 195

Aurora massacre (2012), 127–31, 185

authoritarian personality, 16, 17

authoritarianism, 117, 120, 162

  defined, 162

  of Trump, 27, 31, 32, 152, 158–64, 167, 168, 195, 196, 201

autonomy, 57, 83

  vs. dependency (and caretaking/nurturance), 19, 82–84, 89–90, 94

government as threat to, 83
    See also separation–individuation

Barton, Mark O., 123–25
Being There (film), Chance ("Chauncey Gardiner") in
    compared with Trump, 27–28, 31, 32, 167
    contrasted with Trump, 31, 32, 167
    overview, 27–28, 31
Benedict, Ruth, 15
blogs. *See* writing op-ed pieces (and online blogs)
Boas, Franz, 15
Bolognini, Stefano, 4
Bradley effect, 85
Bush, Billy, 110, 182
Bush, George H. W.
    sexual harassment allegations, 183
    sons' relations with, 8, 55–61, 135
Bush, George W., 9
    Bush administration, 85, 98, 107, 117–19, 145
        Abu Ghraib and the, 143, 145
        America's grandiose persona under the, 116–20
        narcissistic dynamics in the, 115–19
    Iraq policy, 23, 115–20
        grandiose policy of unilateral preemption, 116–18
    9/11 attacks and, 98, 116, 118, 119
    2000 presidential campaign, 19, 55, 61, 80
    relations with George H. W. Bush, 8, 55–61, 135
    relations with Jeb Bush, 23, 62–66, 135
    Saddam Hussein and, 62, 117–19, 145
Bush, Jeb, 23, 57, 62–66, 135

Cash, W. J., 17
"casting couch," 182
castrating, women seen as, 100

Catholic Church, 6–7, 75, 134, 150
Catholics and Donald Trump, 27, 29, 31, 115, 167, 170, 188
censorship, Trump and, 158, 161, 195
Centers for Disease Control and Prevention (CDC), 195, 196
Charlottesville riots, 33, 74, 79, 164, 168
Cheney, Dick, 61, 119
"chosen people," 139
  Jews as, 79, 80, 139
  Serbians as, 139, 141
Clinton, Bill, 23
  Al Gore and, 57–59, 61
  characterizations of, 110
  cooperation between Republicans and Democrats during Clinton
    administration, 25, 26, 30, 165
  criminal allegations against, 71, 108, 110
    impeachment, 7, 70, 179
  denial, 71, 110, 112
  dishonesty, 71, 110, 112, 194
  hatred of, 7, 18, 109, 113
    "Hating the Politician in the Mirror," 68–74
  Hillary Clinton and, 99, 108, 190
  narcissism of minor differences and, 71, 73
  pardons and commutations, 108, 109
  persecution of, 71
  political confessions, 110–12
  public support for, 109, 183–84, 194
  sexual transgressions, 18, 71, 108–13, 157, 182–84, 189, 190, 194
  Trump and, 110, 150, 179
  welfare reform, 97
  See also Sopranos: Clintons compared with
Clinton, Hillary, 63, 99–100, 109–10
  Bill Clinton and, 99, 108, 190
  characterizations of, 99, 110

criminal allegations against, 109, 110, 152

Elizabeth Word Gutting on, 101

email controversy, 102, 114, 194

hatred of, 27, 99–103, 109–10

  misogyny and, 98, 99, 101, 102, 167

2016 presidential campaign, 101–3, 109, 168

Trump and, 99, 101–3, 109, 152, 156, 168, 191, 194

What Happened, 101–2

See also Sopranos: Clintons compared with

cognitive dissonance, 90, 92, 189

Comey, James, 101, 109, 174

compromise. *See under* Democrats and Republicans; United States

Condit, Gary A., 9, 23, 110, 112, 113, 186, 190

confession

  vs. denial, 71, 110, 112, 114, 186–90

  politics of, 111–15, 186–91

conscience. See guilt/remorse and empathy; morality

conservatism, 82–83. *See also* Republicans and Republican ideology

contempt, iv, 74, 109, 116, 117

Crews, Frederick, 44

cult leaders, idealization of, 134

cult of personality, 134, 144, 160

cultural diversity. *See* multiculturalism

culture and personality, 14–15

  causal agents of a culture's personality, 15–16

  configurational approach to, 15

democracy

  dangers of mob mentality in, 160, 168 *(see also* Hamilton, Alexander)

  vs. fascism, 160, 162 *(see also* fascistic authoritarianism of Trump)

  imposing it on other countries, 116, 117, 146

Democratic Party

  symbolizing a suffocating, indulgent mother, 87

symbolizing a warm, nurturing maternal presence, 19, 82
Democrats, 82, 92
   dependency, the need to be taken care of, and, 19, 82–84
Democrats and Republicans, 82–84
   compromise and cooperation between, 25, 30, 80
   gridlock between, 25, 30, 80, 88, 91, 93
   hatred between, 80, 84, 87
      and conflict within America's psyche, 80, 88–90
   polarization of, 97
   See also Republicans and Republican ideology
denial, 114
   Bill Clinton's, 71, 110, 112
   vs. confession, 71, 110, 112, 114, 186–90
   of errors of judgment, 114
   of genocides, 148
   of hatred, 77
   of loved one's faults, 133–35
   projective identification and, 125, 188
   of psychological causation, 53
   psychophobia and, 46, 53 (see also psychophobia)
   of sexual transgressions, 132–34, 184, 186, 187, 190
   Trump's, 87–89, 186–88, 190, 192
   of the unconscious, 46 (see also psychophobia)
   of victims' separate existence, 125
dependency, 107
   vs. autonomy, 19, 82–84, 89–90, 94
   Democrats, the need to be taken care of, and, 19, 82–84
   distrust and avoidance of, 117
   on government
      and personal independence, 97
      and weakness, 94–98
   grandiosity and, 117, 173

healthy, 94, 95, 97, 98
on maternal caretaking, 100, 166
narcissistic fears of, 196
narcissistic personality and, 117, 173, 196
pathological, 95–97
and regression, 95
rugged individualism and, 97
Trump and, 196, 197
See also independence
depressive nihilism. *See* nihilism
"dog-eat-dog world," 117, 158
domination, 118
Dowd, Maureen, 64, 65

Eagleton, Thomas, 5–6, 36–41
psychophobia and, 6, 37–41
ego ideal, 60
Elder, Larry, 129
empathy, 89, 143, 179
aggression, hatred, and, 87, 124, 125, 200
egocentricity and, 117, 124
See also under "other"
envy, 79
of Jews, 78–80
penis, 100
of politicians/political leaders, 112–14, 187
in psychotherapy, 21, 22
Erdoğan, Recep Tayyip, 148
Erikson, Erik H., 16
ethics. See morality; superego; United States
exhibitionist revenge, 143–46
existential anxiety, 128, 130
existential threat(s), 73

"otherness" experienced as, 88
  to white America, 30, 165–66 *(see also* white-lash)
existential trauma, 19
existential vulnerability, 130, 132. *See also* Aurora massacre
exploitative use of others, 32, 118–19

fascism, 161
  vs. democracy, 160, 162
  See also Nazi Germany
fascistic authoritarianism of Trump, 159–64. *See also* under Trump:
personality
father–son relationship, 56–57. *See also* adolescent rebellion; Oedipal
    conflicts; separation–individuation; sibling rivalry
Festinger, Leon, 92
"fiscal cliff," 91–94
Fisher, M., 32, 158, 173, 175, 177
Francis, Pope, 148, 201
Frankel-Brunswick, Else, 16
Franken, Al, 186–88
free speech, Trump and, 158, 161, 195
Freud, Sigmund, 3, 7, 100, 157
  criminality and, 108, 157
  Erik Erikson and, 16
  hate and, 7, 14, 68–70, 72–75, 77, 78
  on history, art, literature, and mythology, 14
  on narcissism of minor differences, 7, 14, 68–70, 72–75
  patients, 21
  on primal horde, 18
  on primary narcissism, 86, 107–8, 166
  on psychological determinism, 53
  psychophobia and, 45–46, 48
  psychosexual stages, 16
  Republicans and, 7, 68–70

on sexual and aggressive impulses, 14, 46, 72, 108, 123, 154–55, 157

structural theory (ego-id-superego), 17

on superego in service of id, 7, 68

traveling exhibit on, 4, 44

writings

    Civilization and Its Discontents, 14, 72, 123, 154

    "On Narcissism," 105, 157

    Totem and Taboo, 14

Freud-bashing, 44–46

Furrow, Buford O., Jr., 124–26

genocide, 14, 70

  use of the term, 148, 149

  See also Armenian Genocide; Holocaust; Serbian genocide

George VI. See *King's Speech*

Germany, 139, 199–200. *See also* Nazi Germany

Gibson, Mel, 77. *See also Passion of the Christ*

Gingrich, Newt, 110, 113

Goldwater, Barry, 22

Goldwater rule, 22–24

  Trump and, 22–24, 198

Gore, Al, Jr., 59–61

  Bill Clinton and, 57–59, 61

  2000 presidential campaign, 19, 55, 57, 59, 61, 80, 135

  relationship with father, 8, 23, 56–61

government, 83

  dependency on, and weakness, 95–98

grandiose self, 158, 197

grandiosity (and self-aggrandizing), 15, 139, 141, 144, 146

  adaptive, 171, 173, 179

  America's grandiose persona under George W. Bush, 116–20

  in childhood, 176

  defensive, 118, 139

maladaptive, 173, 174, 179

narcissistic display of, 116

of Trump, 146, 152, 154, 157, 158, 160, 171–74, 176, 179, 183, 194, 195, 197

See also Aryan race and superiority; "chosen people"; narcissism; nationalism; omnipotence

greed, 79, 125, 155

guilt/remorse and empathy

lack of, 112, 124, 125, 189

See also empathy; Trump, Donald

guns and gun control, 127–32, 184–86

Trump and, 185, 191

Gutting, Elizabeth Word, 101

Hamilton, Alexander, 156, 168

hatred

of "the other," 74, 84–89, 164, 166, 193, 200 *(see also* anti-Semitism; Holocaust)

of women *(see* misogyny)

See also under Clinton, Bill; Clinton, Hillary; Democrats and Republicans; empathy; Freud, Sigmund; narcissism of minor differences; Obama, Barack

Hearst, Patty, 140, 141

Hitler, Adolf, 134, 139, 144, 149, 161, 195. *See also* Nazi Germany

Holmes, James, 131, 132

Holocaust, 70, 78, 149–50, 162

Holocaust denial, 148

honesty, 39, 41. *See also under* Clinton, Bill; Trump, Donald

Huffington, Arianna, 9

Hussein, Saddam. See Saddam Hussein

Hyde, Henry J., 110, 113

idealization, 66, 109, 113, 133

in Bush family, 57, 58, 60, 65, 66, 135

and the corruption of morality, 132–35

grandiosity and, 146

of Joe Paterno, 132, 134 *(see also* Paterno, Joe)

needs served by, 134

of parents, 57, 58, 60, 66, 86, 134, 135 *(see also*
separation–individuation)*

separation–individuation and, 58, 66, 135

of sexual perpetrators, 133–34

of Trump, 146

idealized leader, 161. *See also* Trump, Donald

idealized object, merging with, 132, 134, 161

identification with the aggressor, 43, 140. *See also* Stockholm syndrome

immigration and immigrants

Donald Trump and, 152, 155, 157, 161, 166–70

Muslim, 162, 166, 168, 170, 199

impulse disorders, 124, 126

shift from neuroses to narcissistic and, 123–26

impulsiveness/impulsivity, 107, 121–22, 124

embracing, 107, 124, 155

Freud and, 154–55, 157

narcissistic, 120, 155

treatment, 124, 126

of Trump, 19, 24, 98, 155, 157, 171, 172, 179, 194, 195, 198

independence, 95

George W. Bush and, 59, 61

idealization and, 134

Jeb Bush and, 63

pathological narcissism and, 95

Republicans as representing, 82, 84

separation–individuation and, 59, 65, 135 *(see also*
separation–individuation)*

See also dependency

independent thinking, 163

capacity for, 161
independent women, 99, 100
individualism, rugged, 118
    ethos of, 97, 156
individuation. *See* separation–individuation
infantilism
    of Trump, 152, 157, 171–75, 179, 193
    See also regression
integrity. *See* morality
intergenerational transmission of trauma, 149, 150
Iran, 155
Iran nuclear deal (Joint Comprehensive Plan of Action), 170, 191, 193
Iraq, 155
    George W. Bush and, 23, 115–20
    imposing democracy in, 117, 146
    weapons of mass destruction (WMDs) and, 62, 117, 118
    See also Abu Ghraib torture and prisoner abuse
ISIS (Islamic State of Iraq and Syria), 155
Islam. *See* Muslims
Israel, 80
Trump recognizing Jerusalem as the capital of, 79, 150, 170

Jews
    as "chosen people," 79, 80, 139
    envy of, 78–80
    See also anti-Semitism
Job, Book of, 130

Kardiner, Abram, 15–17
Kelley, Devin B., 184–85
Kernberg, Otto F., 1, 3–4, 21–22, 44
    on narcissism, 197
    on splendid isolation, 159, 197

Kim Jong Un, Trump and, 24, 98, 193–95
King's Speech, The (film), 48, 50–52
Klein, Melanie, 74
Kleinian theory, 79
Kosovo War. *See* Serbian genocide
Kranish, M., 32, 158, 173, 175, 177
Ku Klux Klan (KKK)
  Donald Trump and, 159, 160, 170
  Fred Trump and, 192

Lakoff, George, 18, 19
Lanza, Adam, 131–32
Lasch, Christopher, 155
Lasswell, Harold, 17
law
  regression to vigilante, 186
  using vs. ignoring it to suit one's own purposes, 118–19
Lear, Jonathan, 18
Lee, Bandy, 24
Levinson, David, 16
Levy, Chandra, 9, 23, 62, 110, 112, 190
Lewinsky, Monica S., 71, 110, 112, 113, 182, 189
liberalism, 82. *See also* Democrats
Lincoln, Abraham, 188–89
Linton, Ralph, 15–16
Luther, Martin, 16, 78

malignant normality, 189
managed care, 47
mass shootings, 123–26. *See also* Aurora massacre
maternal representations. *See under* Democratic Party
Mayan apocalypse, 90–92
McCain, John, 84, 85, 87–88, 152
  exhorting party members to work across the aisle, 28, 30

2008 presidential election, 19–20
  on tribal politics, 25, 29, 165
McCarthy, Joseph R., 163
McGovern, George, 6
Mead, Margaret, 15
Mexico, Mexicans, and Donald Trump, 152, 155–57, 161, 166, 170, 174
Milošević, Slobodan, 139, 140, 142
Minutaglio, Bill, 57–60
misogyny, 97, 101, 102, 183, 184
  Freud and, 100
    Hillary Clinton and, 98, 99, 101, 102, 167 *(see also* Clinton, Hillary:
    hatred of)
  worldwide, 100
  See also Trump: attitudes toward women
mob mentality, dangers of, 168
Moore, Roy, 182–88, 190, 200
morality
  compromising America's integrity vs. ensuring military support, 148–50
  idealization and the corruption of, 132–35
  The Mind of Watergate (Rangell), 18, 23, 29, 167
  See also superego; United States
Mueller, Robert, 170, 190, 194
multiculturalism, 27, 28, 30, 31, 115, 165, 168, 200, 201
Muslims, 100, 155
  Albanian, 136, 139–41
  fear of (and white-lash against), 27, 30, 161, 162, 165, 199, 200
  immigration, 162, 166, 168, 170, 199
  Israel, Jews, and, 80
  persecution of, 79–80, 140–42, 201 *(see also* Serbian genocide)
  Trump on, 152, 161, 166, 168, 170, 174, 191, 192
Mussolini, Benito, 17, 160, 161

narcissism
  adaptive, 175
  culture of, 155
  vs. object relatedness, 114
  and the "other," 87, 88, 197, 201
  politics of, 116–20
  primary, 86, 88, 107–8, 166
    See also "chosen people"; Freud, Sigmund; grandiosity;
    omnipotence; Trump: narcissism of
narcissism of minor differences
  and Christian anti-Semitism, 72–75, 77, 78, 80
  Freud on, 7, 14, 68–70, 72–75
  and hatred of "the other," 88, 201
  and the Holocaust, 70
  and protection, strengthening and consolidation of identity, 73
  and Republicans' vitriol, 7, 68–73
  between tribal groups within each political party, 84
narcissistic bloviator
  defined, 154
  irresistible appeal of a, 154–59
narcissistic disorders
  narcissistic personality disorder, 9, 23, 116, 117, 173 (see also grandiose
    self)
  See also under impulse disorders
narcissistic dynamics, 115, 197
  in George W. Bush administration, 115–19
narcissistic injuries/narcissistic wounds, 119, 139, 142, 143, 145
narcissistic regression, 119, 157
Nassar, Larry, 183
  nationalism, 200
  causes of, 199–200
  fascism and, 160
  German, 139, 199–200

right-wing European, 159, 199
    Serbian, 138, 140, 142
    shame, victimhood, and, 139
    Trump and, 158, 159, 161, 199
Nazi Germany, 70, 160. *See also* Holocaust
Nazi physicians, mentality of, 189
Nazis, 17, 168
neutrality, analytic, 20, 21
nihilism, 91, 93
nihilistic despair, 1, 93–94
9/11 terrorist attacks, 2
    Americans' reactions to, 19, 27, 116, 119, 129, 145
    fear of terrorist attacks after, 30, 129, 165
    George W. Bush and, 98, 116, 118, 119
    international reactions to, 118
    and white-lash, 27, 30, 165
Nixon, Richard, 18, 113–14
North Korea
    nuclear weapons, nuclear war, and, 98, 170, 193
    See also Kim Jong Un
North Korea–South Korea relations, 193–94
nuclear weapons and nuclear war
    North Korea and, 98, 170, 193
    Trump and, 98, 170, 193, 194, 198
    See also Iran nuclear deal; weapons of mass destruction

Obama, Barack, 92
    administration, 110, 119
    aggression toward, 87, 191–93
    Armenian Genocide and, 148–50
    citizenship conspiracy theories, iv, 177, 191
    compromising America's integrity vs. ensuring Turkey's military
        support, 147–50

dependency on government and, 94, 95

2008 presidential election, 19–20, 84–88

2012 presidential campaign, 94, 95

race, racism, and, 84–87, 89, 192, 193

Trump and, 177, 185, 191–93

whitelash and, 27, 165–67

Obamacare, 163, 169, 191, 198

object relatedness vs. narcissism, 114. *See also* narcissism

Oedipal conflicts, 14, 18, 58–60

omnipotence

  Bill Clinton's, 109

  children learning that they lack, 107

  defensive fantasies of, 130

  God and, 130

  identification with politicians', 109

  infant's, 88, 107, 108

    mother's "otherness" as threat to, 88

  Jews and, 79

  political power and, 110, 173, 182, 195

  projection of our desire for, 130

  regression to, 110, 131, 173, 182–83

  and sexual transgressions, 182–83

  Trump's, 131, 157, 161, 174, 182–83, 198

O'Neill, Paul, 119

op-ed pieces. *See* writing op-ed pieces

"other" (and "otherness")

  acceptance and embracing of the, 115

  early psychological development and, 86–89

  empathy and identification with the, 87, 166, 168, 200

  fear of the, 87–89, 164, 166, 199–200

  Freud and, 77

  hatred of the, 74, 84–89, 164, 166, 193, 200 *(see also* anti-Semitism;
    Holocaust)

Jews and, 77
loving the, 200, 201
minorities, race, and the, 30, 77, 85–88, 165, 166, 193, 199–201
narcissism and the, 87, 88, 197, 201
2008 presidential election and, 85–89
projection onto the, 74, 75, 87, 89, 110, 197
regression and, 115, 164–66
splitting and, 77
tribalism and, 166, 200
Trump and the, 164, 166, 193, 197, 201
xenophobia and, 30, 168 *(see also* xenophobia)

pardons, 108, 109
Passion of the Christ, The (film), 74–78
Passion Plays, 74, 77
Paterno, Joe, 133, 134, 183
Patient Protection and Affordable Care Act. *See* Obamacare
Paul of Tarsus, Apostle, 74, 76, 77, 96
penis envy, 100
Personal Responsibility and Work Opportunity Reconciliation Act
    of 1996 (PRWORA). *See* Clinton, Bill: welfare reform
phallic power, 100, 186, 193, 198
politicalitis, 1
Powell, Colin, 89, 114
"power corrupts," 115, 151, 182
presidents, U.S.
  with mental disorders, 199
  See also *specific presidents*
primal horde (Freud), 14, 18, 184
projective identification, 201
  anti-Semitism and, 74, 77, 80, 124
  into the "other," 74, 110 *(see also* "other": projection onto the)
  racism and, 87, 124, 125, 141, 201

rage and, 124, 125
of Trump, 188
psychoanalysis, fear of, 43. *See also* Freud-bashing; psychophobia
psychoanalysts' resistance to public media writing, 20–24
psychoanalytic treatment, 20, 21, 124, 126
   non-medical practitioners excluded from practicing analysis, 43–44
psychodynamics, political
   the enduring relevance of, 182–202
   psychodynamic processes, 201–2
psychopathy. *See* guilt/remorse and empathy, lack of
psychophobia, 35–36, 44, 53, 202
   and blaming the mentally ill, 185
   Bush family, "psychobabble," and, 64
   definitions and meanings of the term, 3, 35, 38, 43
   as endemic/ubiquitous, 35, 46, 47
   Freud and, 45–46, 48
   managed care and, 47
   medical schools and, 47
   psychoanalysis and, 4, 43–47
   psychopharmacology and, 47, 48
   stuttering and, 48, 49
   Thomas Eagleton and, 6, 37–41 (*see also* Eagleton, Thomas)
   and the unconscious, 35–36, 43–47, 85
   and voting, 40
   a world of, 45–49
psychosomatic illness, 46
Putin, Vladimir
   Donald Trump and, 26, 29, 167, 170, 194, 197–98

racism
   and hatred of "the other" in 2008 presidential election, 84–88
   projective identification and, 87, 124, 125, 141, 201
   Trump and, 152, 161, 166, 174, 201

See also Ku Klux Klan; Obama, Barack; "other"; white supremacy
Rangell, Leo, 18, 23, 29, 167
  The Mind of Watergate, 18, 23, 29, 167
reason
  vs. tribal politics, 165, 166 (see also white-lash)
  See also science; United States
rebellion against internalized father, 60. *See also* adolescent rebellion
regression, 59, 66
  in American population, 26–31, 115, 119–21, 127, 191
  anti-scientific, 195, 196
  dependency and, 95 *(see also* dependency)
  George W. Bush administration and, 119
  grandiosity and, 173, 182–83
  narcissistic, 119, 157
  to omnipotence, 110, 131, 173, 182–83
  "otherness" and, 115, 164–66
  political, 19, 25–31, 110, 157, 164–68
  power as a stimulant for, 110, 183
  and sexual transgressions, 182–83
  tribal, 26, 28, 29, 165–68, 183, 189, 191
  Trump and, 19, 25–26, 28, 29, 31, 32, 119, 157, 164–68
  to vigilante law, 186
Rendell, Ed, 101
repression, 54–55, 78
Republicans and Republican ideology, 82–83
  autonomy, control, and, 19, 82–84, 89–90
  Freud and, 7, 68–70
  narcissism of minor differences and the vitriol of, 7, 68–73
  as representing independence, 82, 84
  symbolizing a (strict, moralistic) father persona, 19, 83, 89
  See also Democrats and Republicans
revenge

exhibitionist, 143–46

reliance upon revenge in retaliation for injuries to self-esteem, 119

Romney, Mitt, 94, 95

Rumsfeld, Donald, 143, 145

Russia. *See* Putin, Vladimir

Ryan, Paul, 96, 169

Saddam Hussein, George W. Bush and, 62, 117–19, 145

Sanders, Bernie, 99, 101

Sanders, Sarah Huckabee, 187–88

Sandusky, Jerry, 132, 133

Sanford, Nevitt, 16, 17

Schumer, Chuck, 28, 30, 169

Schwartz, Tony, 157–58

science, Trump and, 195–96

Seidler, David, 51

self-aggrandizing. See grandiosity (and self-aggrandizing); narcissism

separation–individuation, 66

  in Bush family, 58, 59, 61–62, 66, 135

  family relationships and, 58, 59, 65, 66, 135

  idealization and, 58, 66, 135

September 11 attacks. *See* 9/11 terrorist attacks

Serbia, 141, 142

Serbian genocide, 137–42

Serbians as "chosen people," 139, 141

Sessions, Jeff, 169, 170

sexual transgressions, 182, 200

  denial of, 132–34, 184, 186, 187, 190

  famous persons accused of, 87, 110, 181–84, 200 *(see also* specific
    individuals)

    of Bill Clinton, 18, 71, 108–13, 157, 182–84, 189, 190, 194 *(see also*
    Lewinsky, Monica S.)

of Donald Trump, 182–83, 190, 198

sibling rivalry

  in Bush family, 60, 62–65

  See also Oedipal conflicts

Silver, Allison, 7, 8, 61–62, 137

social services, 95–97

sociopathy. *See* guilt/remorse and empathy, lack of

Sopranos

  Americans identifying with, 108, 157

  Clintons compared with, 105–9, 157

South Korea. See North Korea–South Korea relations

Spiecker, Gary, 8

Spivak, Alan, 78, 88

splendid isolation, 117, 120, 158, 197

splitting, 26, 30, 74, 80, 94, 135, 165

  defined, 26

  See also idealization

Stalin, Joseph, 134, 144, 197

Starr, Kenneth "Ken" W., 71, 113

Stockholm syndrome, 43, 141. *See also* identification with the aggressor

Stolorow, Robert D., 19

stuttering, as psychological vs. biological, 49–53

superego, 18, 125, 126

  in service of the id, 7, 68, 71

superiority

  America's displays of, 116–17, 119, 139, 161

  and the "other," 86 *(see also* "other")

  threats to one's sense of, 46, 72

  white supremacy and Aryan, 125, 134, 139, 162, 195 *(see also* Ku Klux
    Klan)

  See also "chosen people"; grandiosity; nationalism

terrorism. *See* 9/11 terrorist attacks

torture. *See* Abu Ghraib torture and prisoner abuse

transference, 21–22

trauma

existential, 19

intergenerational transmission of, 149, 150

tribal politics, 25–28, 189, 200

John McCain on, 25, 29, 165

Trump and, 25–28, 30–31, 166

See also narcissism of minor differences

tribal regression, 26, 28, 29, 165–68, 183, 189, 191

Trump, Donald, 12, 150

attitudes toward women, 101, 152

Access Hollywood tape, *110, 182–83*

Bill Clinton and, 110, 150, 179

Chance ("Chauncey Gardiner") in *Being There* compared with, 27–28, 31, 32, 167

characterizations of, 24, 193

childhood, 158, 177–79

criminal allegations against, 19, 170, 172–74, 177, 179, 190, 199

sexual transgressions, 182–83, 190, 198

denial, 87–89, 186–88, 190, 192

deprecating labels used by, iv, 152

education, 158, 177–79

ethics, morality, conscience and, 19, 115, 152, 165

exploitative strategy, 32

family background, 175–78, 192

Goldwater rule and, 22–24, 198

Hillary Clinton and, 99, 101–3, 109, 152, 156, 168, 191, 194

influence on the American psyche, 1, 25–26

Israel and, 79, 80, 150

Kim Jong Un and, 24, 98, 193–95

and the media, 152, 153, 161, 163, 172, 174

Mexico, Mexicans, and, 152, 155–57, 161, 166, 170, 174
narcissism of, iii–iv, 23, 26, 98, 110, 115, 119, 146, 151–52, 160 *(see also under* grandiosity; omnipotence)
   as a key to his success and tragic flaw, 172–79
   the strange, irresistible appeal of a narcissistic bloviator, 154–59
nationalism and, 158, 159, 161, 199
at New York Military Academy, 158, 177–79
nuclear weapons, nuclear war, and, 98, 170, 193, 194, 198
Obamacare and, 191, 198
personality, iv, 19, 24, 152, 155, 171, 172, 177–79, 198, 201
   (fascistic) authoritarianism, 27, 31, 32, 152, 158–64, 167, 168, 195, 196, 201
   authenticity, 155
   impulsiveness, 19, 24, 98, 155, 157, 171, 172, 179, 194, 195, 198
   phallic power and competitiveness, 193, 198
   superiority, 146, 152
policies, iv, 19, 26–27, 29, 161, 166–71, 185, 191, 195–99
   immigration, 166–70 *(see also* under immigration and immigrants)
political behavior, iv, 19, 25–26, 146, 152, 168, 173–74, 190–91, 195, 196
   revenge against Obama, 191–94
2016 presidential campaign, 151–52
2016 presidential victory, 119, 168
psychoanalyzing and psychological assessment of, 11, 20, 22–24, 151–52, 202
psychopathology, 24, 152, 170–71, 198, 199
   ADHD, 158
   infantilism, 152, 157, 171–75, 179, 193
   narcissistic personality disorder, 23
   race, racism, and, 152, 161, 166, 174, 201
   reactions to the presidency of, 1, 19, 20
   regression and, 19, 25–26, 28, 29, 31, 32, 119, 157, 164–68
   supporters of, iv, 26–29, 31, 32, 102, 115, 154, 166–67, 170, 199, 200

tribal politics and, 25–28, 30–31, 166
truthfulness and, 155 (see also science)
   dishonesty and false claims, iv, 169, 174, 177, 191, 192, 195, 196
unsuitability for the presidency, 24, 152, 198, 199
Vladimir Putin and, 26, 29, 167, 170, 194, 197–98
whitelash of, 201–2
Trump, Fred "Freddy" (Donald's brother), 178
Trump, Frederick Christ "Fred" (Donald's father), 175, 178, 192
Trump, Mary Anne MacLeod (Donald's mother), 175–76
Twain, Mark, 59, 65–66

unconscious psychodynamics, 201–2
   denial of, 46 *(see also* psychophobia)
Unite the Right rally (Charlottesville rally), 33, 74, 79, 164, 168
United States
   healthy and divided state of mind, 81–84
   regressive politics and loss of reason, ethics, and compromise, 29–33
   See also *specific topics*

victimhood, politics of, 138–42. *See also* Abu Ghraib torture and
   prisoner abuse
violence
   mass, 123–26 *(see also* Aurora massacre)
   See also guns and gun control
Volkan, Vamik D., 18, 141

Watergate scandal, 18
   The Mind of Watergate (Rangell), 18, 23, 29, 167
weapons of mass destruction (WMDs)
   Iraq and, 62, 117, 118
   See also nuclear weapons and nuclear war
Welch, Jack, 52
welfare reform, 97

white-lash, 27, 30, 33, 115, 165–70
  9/11 attacks and, 27, 30, 165
  Obama and, 27, 165–67
  Trump's, 201–2
white supremacy, 125, 134, 139, 162, 195. *See also* Aryan race and
  superiority; Ku Klux Klan
witch hunts, 129, 163, 184
Wizard of Oz, The (film), 146
Wolson, Peter
  background for political writing, 4–11
  patients' reactions to reading his publications, 21
  writing process, 25–28 *(see also* writing op-ed pieces)
women
  independent, 99, 100
  seen as castrating, 100
  See also misogyny; Trump: attitudes toward women
World War II, 149, 197. See also Holocaust; Nazi Germany
writing op-ed pieces (and online blogs)
  and America's regressive politics, 29–33
  historical precedent, 14–20
  psychoanalysts' resistance to public media writing, 20–24
  Wolson's writing process, 25–28
  See also under Wolson, Peter

xenophobia, 30, 31, 165, 168, 200. *See also* "other"

Zakaria, Fareed, 199
Zaretsky, Eli, 17

ABOUT THE AUTHOR

Peter Wolson, Ph.D. is a training and supervising
analyst and faculty member of the *Los Angeles Institute and Society For
Psychoanalytic Studies*. He has served as *LAISPS'* President and Director
of Training, is a co-founding member of the *Confederation of Independent
Psychoanalytic Societies* and was President of the Los Angeles Society
of Clinical Psychologists. He is on the resident faculty of the Wright
Institute Los Angeles and in private practice in Beverly Hills. In addition to his political opinion pieces, he has published professional papers
on adaptive grandiosity, the existential dimension of psychoanalysis, the
relational unconscious, analytic love and political power.